Pitch Uncertain

Maisie Kinnicutt *by Gardner Cox, c. 1952*

Pitch Uncertain

A MID-CENTURY MIDDLE DAUGHTER FINDS HER VOICE

Maisie Houghton

TIDEPOOL PRESS
Cambridge, Massachusetts

Published in the United States in 2011 by TidePool Press

For information, address TidePool Press
6 Maple Avenue, Cambridge, Massachusetts 02139
www.tidepoolpress.com

Printed in the United States

Library of Congress Cataloging-in-Publication Data

Houghton, Maisie, 1940-
     Pitch Uncertain: A Mid-century Middle Daughter Finds Her Voice
     p.cm.
     ISBN 0-9755557-6-7/978-0-9755557-6-7
     1. Houghton, Maisie 2. Cambridge—United States—Biography
     3. Radcliffe College 4. Dark Harbor—Maine
     I. Title.

     2010938244

To my sisters

TABLE OF CONTENTS

Acknowledgments

GROWING UP—which is the essence of this story—there was a ritual made of saving the Sunday lunch roast chicken wishbone. You made a wish, shut your eyes tight, held this dry little Y-shaped bone in one hand, while the other piece of the downturned Y was held by a friend, in my case usually a sister. You pulled tight against each other and whoever ended up with the longer section "won." Your wish would be granted. Recently someone told me that is where the expression "lucky break" came from.

All my life I have been lucky.

To start with, I have been lucky to meet the publishers of TidePool Press. The brothers Herron, Jock and Frank, are most astute and tactful editors while Ingrid Mach transposes ordinary family photographs into elegant art.

I began to write these pages as part of a class at the West Side Y on West 63rd Street in NYC. There I met a gifted teacher, Patty

Dann, who told me to "string my sketches together like pieces of a fan." I am grateful to Patty and also to Marion Landew and Sally Arteseros, who gave me good advice along the way.

Mary Buechner, Robin van Löben Sels and Anstiss Hammond Krueck have also given me different varieties of help.

On the home front, I owe a lot to Steve Blackwell and Carol Pease, who always kept life around me serene and ordered—so that there were no excuses not to write.

Terry Austin and Tracie Makowiec have been invaluable to me, skilled as they are in all matters technical, not one of my strong points.

My sisters are, of course, the backbone of this story—even if they might not have wished for it. Sadly, Tizzy did not live to see this book in print but I hope she would have accepted it with her customary grace and discerning eye.

My debt to Sybil Baldwin is enormous. She has kept her sense of humor as she read this story even as she has gently reminded me that every family member sees the same situation, its facts and faces, differently.

Happily, though I know she would tell another kind of story as I wrote mine, Sybil has been a generous, steadfast source of support and encouragement. She is the wisest of sisters and the greatest of friends.

And to Jamie Houghton, with me the proud parent of James DeKay and Nina Houghton, devoted parent-in-law of Connie Coburn and Kent George, exuberant grandfather of Isabelle and Abigail Houghton, Finn and Augusta George, I thank for almost fifty years of witty and loving imperturbability.

Pitch Uncertain

Pitch Uncertain

I WAS BORN IN 1940, a bad time for the world, but I never did anything bad until the day I cut off my hair and left it on the floor for my mother to find, a bright, hot pool of yellow curls.

I was four. It was wartime and we were living in a rented house in Winter Park, Florida. My father, an officer in the navy, had recently been stationed there. My mother and I, along with Sybil, my older sister by two years, and Elizabeth, "Tizzy," a new baby of two months, had moved from New York City to be near him.

Florida, despite all its palm trees and relentless sunlight, seemed dark to me—the people and the houses. Unaccustomed to southern heat, my mother kept the old, verandaed house heavily shaded. The blinds were always down, the curtains drawn. Someone was always taking a nap, my mother, my father (but not together), the amorphous baby. Sybil and I tiptoed around the closed doors, but when we went outside the glittering light hurt our eyes.

In the kitchen was Lily Mae, the black maid. Marion Skillon, a trained nurse from Naples, Maine, was also there. Uncertain in a new land, my mother had persuaded Marion to make the long journey south. Marion, all starched whiteness and squeaking rubber-soled shoes, stuck to the new baby upstairs. Lily Mae ironed endless rivers of laundry and passed dead-looking platters of food in the shadowy dining room.

My father was almost never there. When he did appear, it was often with a swirl of laughing young pilots in uniform. They brought us shells from the beach that we never visited. They set us on their knees, putting down their drinks to balance us on their laps.

The afternoon I rebelled, my mother was a long while on the telephone. She wasn't the type to chatter on. She served as a sounding board to solve other people's problems. My mother had been called to the telephone during a rare treat: We had been having lunch alone together. Her low voice burred on as she twisted the cord in her hand. What was she saying? To whom was she speaking?

I slipped away from the dining room table, wandering sulkily through the muted rooms. On my mother's desk a pair of scissors gleamed. Long and sleek, they were grown ups' scissors, not the stubby, disappointingly blunt ones we used for paper dolls. I ran my hand over my head. My hair was the one thing about me that was different. In everything else I matched my sister—our seersucker dresses, our red sandals, our black eyes. But Sybil had two brown pigtails while I still had a baby's fuzz of buttery curls. I thought about Marion Skillon in the mornings, twisting my hair into ringlets, wrestling the ribbon to the top of my head. "There now, aren't you sweet? Now go and be good."

Suddenly it was easy to pick up the slender weapon and start to cut. One tentative snip and then I was possessed with the necessity to act and be done with my boldness. My curls fell away like skin being shed by a snake. It went so fast I hardly knew what I was doing. I crept back to the kitchen to face Lily Mae. She stared silently. "Your mama be upset," she said, shaking her head as she moved through the swinging door with a stack of freshly ironed shirts. A little panic seized me, but, almost gleefully, I hurried to stand defiantly before my mother. She was still sitting, unspeaking, by the telephone. She seemed unmoved. "Heavens, what did you do that for? It will take forever to grow out." Marion peered at me over the banister railing. "You've lost your looks," she sniffed.

My mother guided me toward the dining room. "We must finish lunch," she murmured, rousing herself. The table looked half-ravaged, like my hair, with crumpled napkins and tired lettuce on the plates. I started to weep at the enormity of what I had done. Fat tears fell on my grilled cheese sandwich. "Don't fuss, darling," consoled my mother distractedly. She wasn't even looking at me.

—⚭—

There was an unspoken lesson in that afternoon. My mother should have been angry but instead she held her tongue. Was it at that point that I learned to guard the peace, to mind my manners, to keep my mouth shut?

On my report card, the music teacher wrote "pitch uncertain."

In school someone would grab me from behind on the playground: "whose side are you on? Lucy's?"—the charismatic troublemaker, or "Kitten's?"—the charismatic good-girl. It seemed easier—and smarter—to keep my mouth shut.

One day I came home from school tense, weepy from trying to please everyone. My mother uncharacteristically drew herself up and exhorted me to "Stick by your guns, have the courage of your convictions." Most important of all, "Be yourself!"

"But how do I know who I am?" I wondered.

Growing up, I swam like a fish in the clouded waters of family life.

My family was large, consisting mostly of women. Since I was born in 1940, the men in the family were soon absent, sent as soldiers to Europe or as naval officers aboard ships to the distant Pacific.

I remember not only my mother's mother, "Gran," as we called her, but also her mother, my great-grandmother, erect, dignified and austere in her long dress. The family I remember also harbored a great-great maiden aunt, several great-aunts and endless pretty cousins. During the war we stayed intermittently with my mother's mother, Gran Jay. Though a young widow at fifty-two, she still kept a rambling house in what was then the quiet countryside of Long Island for her five daughters and one neighboring daughter-in-law.

Gran ran her house as an ark, the center of an otherwise fragmented family life. Her daughters dipped in and out of this comfortable, familiar world, using it as a kind of sacred place,

The Jay sisters with their mother, 1932

sometimes for absolution and redemption, sometimes just for temporary sustenance, always for nourishment.

I fed upon the scraps of long-ago family lore: great-grandmother Kane, whose hair was so long she could sit on it; great-great Aunt Sybil, who showed us her brother's mother-of-pearl handled pistol, a relic of his days with the Rough Riders; and the epic tale of great-great-great- (the "greats" piled up like layers of a cake, staggering in the eternity they suggested) grandfather

Morgan, who walked barefoot from Hartford to Boston to save his shoe leather.

I heard these stories as my two sisters and I traveled with my mother. During the war we always seemed to be moving, on a train crowded with soldiers, or waiting in a station. When my mother saved up enough ration cards for gasoline, we three little girls were squeezed into the backseat of her dusty car. We were going to the next faraway base to see my father, an enigmatic figure in his uniform of khaki shirt and trousers to match. He also wore a jaunty wedged-shaped cap that perched on his tan, handsome, slightly balding head.

He always met us with the same greeting. "You girls are getting so big; I can't remember how old you are." We adored being thought big, grown-up, worldly. Then came his favorite joke (because my father right away wanted to be thought amusing.)

"Why did the three little strawberries cry?" (Long, suspenseful pause while we two older ones gathered gleefully around him because, of course, we knew the answer.)

"Because their mother was in a jam."

And then he was off again, laughing, rumpling our hair, tweaking our dress sashes, but off, away, gone—to war, to a bar, to somebody else.

It took me a long time to sort out the differences and navigate the divide between my parents, the two gods of my childhood. They seemed so opposite, so diametrically opposed. Yet to look at them together, they appeared to share so much.

My parents and their families lived in comfort, not excessive luxury, but with gardens and guest rooms, pantries and linen

*My mother, Sybil Jay, and my father, Francis Parker Kinnicutt,
c. 1942*

closets. The men went to college, usually Harvard, and the women did not, but they knew how to do things like draw and ride horseback. As decent, cultivated people they traveled to Europe and treated their servants well. They tried to think beyond their small world. But mostly they toed the line. Born in an age dominated by Victorian culture, they stuck close to the eastern seaboard of the United States as healthy, humble WASPs.

My mother, Sybil, was born in 1914 as something she never forgot: a Jay. The Jays were French Huguenots from the Île de Ré, an island off the west coast of France, near La Rochelle. The Jay men came to this country in the seventeenth century and settled primarily around New York City as farmers, merchants, ministers, lawyers. Then, the family story goes, they took to marrying rich women and never had to work for a living again. But the Jays were also serious, high-minded idealists. One of their early ancestors was John Jay, first chief justice of the Supreme Court. My grandfather Delancey Kane Jay, a classmate of Franklin Roosevelt at Groton and Harvard (my grandfather considered the young Franklin a prig and a fop), trained as a lawyer, won a Distinguished Service Cross in World War I for bravery at Château du Diable, near Fismes, France, started a small family trust company still in existence today, and was among the first to urge America back into war in the defense of Great Britain and a Europe threatened by the Nazis. All this I heard from my mother in hushed, reverential tones. Lanny Jay died of a weak heart at age fifty-nine in 1941, a few months after I was born.

My father, Francis Parker Kinnicutt, came from less grand stock, but the genes were much the same: the same industrious citizens, farmers, bankers, doctors, the same literate, prosperous, politely call-paying people.

My Kinnicutt grandparents had their antecedents in New England, but they chose to live in New York City. It was a propitious choice. From New England, they brought Yankee thrift and a Puritan ardor for hard work and discipline. Life in New York City suited them, with its seductive realization of an abundance of opportunity and pleasure. My grandfather G. Hermann Kinnicutt did well on Wall Street. He founded his own firm, Kissel, Kinnicutt & Co., nothing unusual then but noteworthy for a country doctor's son from Worcester, Massachusetts. My father, born in 1908, never wanted to exert himself on this big stage. He was perhaps lazy, tentative, or just anxious, but he preferred to arrange life according to his own way. As a reaction to Hermann's dedicated work ethic, my father, Frankie, eased into the casual mode of a 1920s spoiled playboy and ended up a Peter Pan.

When Frankie met Sybil, my mother, he was a few years out of Harvard College where his life had centered mostly on high jinks at the Porcellian Club, a fraternity of similarly spoiled and glamour-struck youth. (While he was at Harvard, his mother, fretting yet indulgent, had engaged a taxi to track him wherever he wandered so that there was never a question of his drinking and driving.) In 1935 he was a reluctant student at Columbia Law School, while my mother was taking courses at Barnard College. He saw her on a double-decker bus and persuaded her to sit with him in the top section while they wound their rumbly way up Broadway to 112th Street. They married in February of 1937 and for a honeymoon, Frankie took Sybil to Wyoming for the skiing, something he loved to do but did badly while she, the novice but natural athlete, learned to ski very well.

How my parents met was a story I loved to hear but it was never a mystery, for how could they not have met? Years later a friend showed me a slim book she had found among her family papers. It was a list of the members of the Thursday Evening Club in New York City, and among those members are both sets of my grandparents, the parents of various godparents, the odd great-aunt and uncle. The club's bylaws described it as being a "meeting ground of intellectuality and affability," bringing together "a few kindred spirits interested in the arts, literature, music and science, and equally important, possessed of the social graces." The club never met during Lent.

Thus my parents found each other almost by predestination. Like storybook figures, they had once been in love but then drifted into the lonely estrangement that was to mark my growing-up years. Their unhappiness cast me into a kind of mild imprisonment of yearning and tension.

In the marriage, my mother led, not by dominance, but by passivity. She was always there to pick up the pieces. Sybil Jay had been born the gentle doe of a country-gentry family with a glamorous father herself. It never occurred to her to say "no" or "I want" or even "I." She was the Cinderella in our house, not only physically doing all the work—cooking our meals, driving the carpool, mowing the lawn—but morally holding the fort against the dazzling prince, my father.

My father was quick-silver, brilliant, elusive, with a fountain of friends, buddies and sweethearts, while my mother stood for decorum, convention and security. Her imprint was firm. We daughters adored her, wanting to protect her from this errant Pied Piper, her husband. Witty, irreverent, mercurial, he never got over being his mother's favorite. Good-looking to the point of flashy, with black hair and green eyes, he was forever part of the Martini Generation, and one drink would set him off. One never knew in what direction, whether on a reel of funny stories or into a flash of temper. Never very mature, always appealing, he was a confused and confusing father.

But if the memory of my father is in high relief, the memory of my mother is as the underside of an intaglio: smooth and bright on the surface, underneath deep, powerful, the negative force. A stern guardian of her three daughters, she kept us as reined in and checked as she held herself.

Still, I liked playing my cards close to my chest. I was the middle of three, forever observing, silently absorbing the family scene.

At home, after school, at the end of the afternoon, I would often find my grandmother and mother talking to each other over the tea tray in low, confiding tones. I pressed close to them,

Tizzy, Sybil and Maisie, c. 1947

happy they were together, for once sitting down in peace. Their strong, knobby, long-fingered hands were the same, as they drew teacups to their lips, laid aside reading glasses and knitting needles, or gave the last polish to the crossword puzzle. They each revered the other and could never see enough of each other: my widowed grandmother often away on restless travels, my dutiful mother so engulfed in household responsibilities.

As I approached, the conversation would fade off. "Least said, soonest mended," my grandmother would murmur and a dark eyebrow would arch ever so slightly. I burrowed nearer and pretended to read my book. If I was quiet for long enough, those consoling voices would resume, and I would find out something interesting. Some baffling, unconnected piece of information would float out of their mysterious circle of talk and lodge itself in my consciousness, like a dust speck in the eye. Someone was leaving, someone was coming home, someone was unhappy but she would get over it because she was so young.

I was hooked on the grown-up world.

A Silver Spoon in Its Mouth

DURING THE WAR MY SISTERS and I were shuttled back and forth between two sets of grandparents. My Kinnicutt grandparents lived in a dark, perfect house called Mayfields in Far Hills, New Jersey, where everything matched. My grandfather collected early American furniture while my grandmother was a crack bridge player. Apparently, in the midst of a game she would put down her cards and demand, "Who was she?" as the company chattered on about some wayward friend or child of an acquaintance. The correct lineage noted, she would pick up her hand and resume play without missing a beat.

My grandparents were hardly ever present in their immaculate house in the country. As they grew older they preferred their Park Avenue apartment, being nearer as it was to their clubs and their doctors. Still, they liked the idea someone was "using" what they had worked so hard to perfect. At supper time alone by ourselves in the house empty of anyone but servants, we little girls were served creamed chicken in the maids' dining

Elizabeth Jay, "Gran," c. 1944

room. Upstairs, down a long narrow hall, we once found a large, gangly Charlie McCarthy doll propped up on a bed. He was as exquisitely dressed and as disappointingly silent as my absent Kinnicutt grandparents.

Naturally (and perhaps unfairly because she was so obviously my mother's preference), my grandmother Jay won our allegiance hands down. From the moment we walked through the door into her Long Island house, it was fun. Gran ran toward us, arms outstretched, a trio of small dogs yapping at her feet, a hairpin or two falling from her extravagant pompadour of fading auburn hair. Considered a beauty in her day with her repoussé nose and shining hazel eyes, she was now a bit disheveled. Her stockings crumpled slightly around her ankles, her lipstick ran a little awry as she usually had applied it while driving in her lurching Buick station wagon.

Everything in the house was also just slightly off center. Lampshades, heavy with dust, sagged under the pull of silk fringe. Swatches of chintz or brocade were draped across the backs of oversize armchairs, as Gran could never quite decide which cover, the old threadbare one or the new rosy sample, she liked best. In the sunny dining room facing the broad south lawn, one of her many ancient dogs was always being sick under the dining room table. In the center of the round mahogany table was a silver tankard. The lid never shut properly because the tankard itself was stuffed with well-thumbed bread-and-butter letters, so called because they were written to express thanks for my grandmother's hospitality.

"Dear Mrs. Jay, What a wonderful time I had, how kind you were to have me out last weekend. Sybil's party was lots of fun. I thought it so amusing to sit at table and read all the old bread-and-butter letters."

Gran was full of paradoxes. Raised in a conventional, Old World style, she herself was unconventional. Her parents inhabited a kind of Never Never Land, the last stand of a turn of the century enclave of harmless beings who lived, however naively, for pleasure and leisure. Of all the stories about her family told to me by my mother, tall tales or not, none seemed more fabulous than the ones about her grandfather, Edwin Denison Morgan. It all started with the story of this legendary grandfather as a little boy being hauled out of bed one night in Albany where he lived with his grandfather, who was then governor of New York. The president of the United States, none other than Abraham Lincoln, was coming to dinner. There were thirteen at table so this superstition dictated that this sleepy boy of eight or nine go downstairs to join the party. (By now, we sisters were familiar with the outcome of the story: how Lincoln asked the little boy what he wanted to be when he grew up. "An officer in the United States Army" was the answer, and Lincoln wrote out the commission then and there.)

For us hearing these stories, great-grandfather Morgan, my mother's grandfather, my Gran's father burgeoned into some kind of flourishing Midas figure. He became the symbol of long-gone family wealth and excess. (My cousins and I are still dividing up blue-bordered china soup plates; I still use expansive white damask table napkins; every item—plate and linen—is monogrammed "EDM.") As the sole heir of his grandfather, the governor, Edwin inherited a nice chunk of money as a young man. The money came from a humble start, a grocery store in Hartford, then a slew of timely investments. Perhaps the most daring of Governor Morgan's business ventures was his purchase of cattle ranches in Mexico. But in that boldness was also the beginning of the end of any family fortune, as the land was later seized by the famous Mexican revolutionary Emiliano Zapata.

Grandpa Morgan, as my mother called him, was a bon vivant and a sportsman. He threw himself not into the wise business investments of his grandfather the governor, but into living well. This meant big houses, big horses for fox hunting and big boats for racing off the coast of Newport.

I'm sure my great-grandparents were decent people, certainly genial and kind, and devoted to their children, especially their favorite, Elizabeth, my grandmother. Yet they were part of that tiny elite class where no one had a job and "everyone" had a yacht. There was no income tax and Europe was viewed as a personal playground for sport and parties. Of course this lavishness was to end abruptly, but I imagine many good fairies creeping into my grandmother's mythical christening party. She seemed blessed by every good fortune: adoring family and infectious charm, along with plenty of money and a pretty face, but there must also have been an impudent gremlin who hissed in her innocent ear, "May you always do exactly as you please." Because that was exactly what she did.

Educated at home (until as a teenager she finally was sent to the Brearley School in New York City), taught to ride and sail, to draw and recite poetry, Gran seemed oblivious to the extravaganzas of her youth. After all, it was my mother who told us these elaborate stories. I never heard my grandmother mention her glamorous father.

She used to say that "cellar door" were her favorite words in the English language. She liked the poetry of the phrase, but I suspect it was the earthy, pleasant place that it evoked, that pleased her most. Out in the kennel was where she was happiest, stirring up a special gruel for a sick dog, helping with the birth of a new puppy. She avoided tiresome household responsibilities so that her patient husband was the one who checked out the larder, hired the cook and worried about dust balls under the bed. When she married Lanny Jay in 1910, she kept her own name Elizabeth Sarah, instead of adopting the custom of the time and referring back to her maiden name. She was born a Morgan, though only distantly related to the grand potentate (apparently my great-grandfather loved the barroom song, "My name is Morgan but it ain't J.P."). Thus Elizabeth Sarah remained a kind of free spirit, all her long life, eschewing the propriety, the status even of her family name.

Once we arrived at her house in Westbury on Long Island, a sense of circus never stopped. Gran usually wore a denim apron wrapped around her widening waist. A string of pearls was her constant ornament. After hugging us, she would plop her ever-present tumbler of chocolate milk on the top of the mahogany music box that dated from her childhood. We children gathered around to watch as she cranked it up. As I gazed, enchanted, through the small windowpane of the massive, coffin-like chest, the music box creaked into action. Odd metal disks began to grind their jagged-tooth edges. Fat cylinders stuck with rows of spiny prickles slowly churned round and round. Pert sticks of steel struggled to rat-a-tat-tat on the shiny smooth surface of a silver drum. A faint echo of Strauss' *Blue Danube* bleated out into the drafty hall.

Movement and light were keystones of Gran's domain. It could

*My mother and cousin Temple Morgan with me on the lawn
of Gran's house on Long Island, c. 1943*

have been a sad time. The war was on; everyone's husband,
brother, lover or son was far away in battle. My grandfather Jay
had dropped dead of a heart attack a few years earlier. Gran's
own father had also recently died. Granny Morgan, his widow,
moved to a gardener's cottage on the grounds of the large estate
which was put up for sale. She remained a sober presence in our
lives with her lined visage and black dresses drooping to the
floor. But Gran continued radiant despite these tragedies. All
her life she had been surrounded with love. Now she gave it back
in abundance.

The phone was always ringing in this house. The youngest daughter, teenage Aunt Kitty, would push us out of the way as we played our card game of pounce on the floor. "I'll get it; I'll get it," she would cry. One day when she came back from the telephone in its little perch in the "office" where the dogs' meals were mixed, she spun me out by the arms. Whirling me around in exuberant circles, she explained about some current suitor, "He's coming to tea, now you can meet him."

Tea at my grandmother's was a daily ritual. Gran liked to sit in the West Room to enjoy the last mellow light of afternoon. Jean Whiteford, the aging Scottish housekeeper, would shuffle in with a tray laden with stacks of flowered cups and saucers, a battered teapot of silver and a plate of cinnamon toast cut in triangles. Anyone who was home at that hour usually ended up in that spacious room. Gran sat in the middle of the sofa, in front of the tea tray; using one hand she filled teacups, with the other she absently fed scraps of stale fruit-cake to the dogs. For us children it was cups of the mostly milk of cambric tea.

After tea, she read to us from her favorite picture book of childhood about the Golliwoggs. We dunked sugar cubes into the remains of the teacups and sucked them noisily as we listened to Gran intone the familiar story in her low, confiding voice, made huskier by the quantities of cigarettes she puffed on and then threw away. "Oh, don't ever smoke, it's a disgusting habit," she would remind us as she searched through her floppy handbag for matches.

As we straggled out of the room, we lingered for one last ritual. In a corner was a glass cabinet crammed with knickknacks, tiny china figurines of a shepherdess in a straw hat, tortoiseshell boxes, a gold-colored vial with a chain attached. Gran explained that this was a party favor she had once received at a dance. A suitor would send flowers; you would put them in the vial and pin it to the sash around your waist. "I never knew any boys until I was eighteen," insisted Gran. "I was so shy I just hid away with my brothers."

Even as a child I recognized how pretty and flirtatious my grandmother was. There is a portrait of her as a young woman of about twenty: she is dressed for a party in gauzy white tulle which falls decorously from her bare shoulders. Her mass of thick curls is crowned with a wreath of holly. Eyes downcast, she looks modestly at her clasped hands. But the corners of her mouth are curling up, aching to burst into a coquettish smile.

Gran let us each choose a present from the case. "Just one, Mom," instructed my mother piously. I stood for an agonizing moment, hesitating between a fat lead duck tucked under a red umbrella, or a carved mother-of-pearl stamp case. Gran whispered, "Choose one now and I'll sneak you the other one later."

Gran doted on family. It was the idea of home, peace, familiarity rather than any unique, separate individual that appealed to her. She had loved her husband, a straight-backed, aloof stranger we never knew. Now she fussed over her six children, her beguiling, alcoholic brothers, her stately mother who brought up her daughter never to read a novel in the morning (definitely not a dictum Gran followed). Close in her affections came her innumerable dogs, from Chihuahua puppies named Frito and Cheezit (Gran's favorite food) to bounding black briard sheepdogs.

Portrait of Elizabeth Morgan by Lydia Field Emmet, 1907

Supposedly the dogs lived in outlying sheds or barns, but two or three Pekinese were often found curled up on a sofa while an overweight dachshund, named Little Lulu (Gran's favorite comic strip), slept with Gran in her bed.

In a time of both personal and universal loss, with the war raging around the world, beyond the quiet, leafy confines of this country house, Gran was a lively reminder of continuing vitality. One of her offhand treasures was a silver spoon engraved with a drawing of the Charles McKim house her parents had been building when she was born. Now she lived on the edge of this once-grand property. The house was long shut and deserted, and would soon be sold. Still inscribed on the slender handle of the silver spoon was the prophetic phrase, "born with a silver spoon in its mouth," the giver apparently unaware of the sex of the child to whom he wanted to give this present.

Gran was born in 1889. By 1944 when I was four, much had been lost—the family fortune shrunk, her winsome beauty faded, and her beloved husband dead for three years. When I first began to admire and need her, Gran was plump and gray but she didn't seem to care. The money she had was plenty for her; she reveled in her passion for her dogs, songbirds and her family (in which order was perhaps a bone of contention for her daughters). When she was fed up with her macaw or the cockatoo, she threw a fraying towel over its cage. That shut them up. She could then move on to the next project, the next sagging porch she wanted to restore, the next radio program she wanted to listen to, the next Top 10 tune she wanted to whistle. Amidst all the topsy-turvy, makeshift arrangements of her daily life, all the milk glasses that were forgotten and slid off the top of her moving car, all the misplaced eyeglasses and unbalanced checkbooks, Gran was accomplished in the art of living in the moment, something the rest of her progeny had difficulty mastering.

Women Without Men

My MOTHER, HER MOTHER, her sisters and my sisters formed the fortress of my early years. Life at the Long Island house blurs over now, but the memory of the place lulls me into an indulgent romance of comfort and security.

The last time I was ever to visit was in 1945. The war was just over, a family of soldiers had come home and Gusty, one of my young aunts, was to be married at my grandmother's house on Long Island. My mother brought her young brood of little girls to spend the weekend before the wedding in her old family home.

There were five Jay daughters: Betsy, the firstborn, brilliantly blue-eyed and imperious as the oldest, forever in charge; Sybil, my mother, self-effacing and obliging, thus everyone's favorite; Theo, a grave dark-haired beauty who loved life but had trouble being happy. These three sisters were already married with varying degrees of success. The bride, Augusta, called Gusty by everyone, as that was exactly what she was—fresh, frank and lively—had been an army nurse, pursued by many admirers.

Augusta Jay, "Aunt Gusty," c. 1944

But she had finally relented to an old Groton School friend of her brother's, Huston Huffman, who was moving west to take a gamble on the oil business in Texas. Kitty was the "baby," a high-spirited teenager who wrapped her widowed mother around her little finger.

The wedding took place a month before Christmas. The family was rallying in droves, as Texas seemed an impossibly faraway place for Gusty to roost. The night before the wedding was a party of only family, "just us," as Gusty insisted she wanted it to be. No groom, no husbands, no men as far as I remember. My mother and her sisters gathered in the big West Room, smoking, sipping bourbon and soda. I had never seen my mother so carefree and relaxed.

I begged to be allowed to stay up for this last night of all the sisters together. I hung over my mother's shoulder, burrowing into her lap, pleading, "Let me stay, don't make me go to bed." I loved being folded into the warmth of those pretty women. Loose sweaters smelling faintly of perfume dangled from their shoulders, their slim legs were crossed, a high-heeled shoe flopped on and off and then was snapped back again. One red-lacquered nail slowly swirled a watery ice cube. It was the sisters at ease, cozy with each other, those five women who only felt truly comfortable at home. Even Gran, their irrepressibly lively mother, had been packed off to sleep. But finally even my patient mother turned on me. "Up, May-Day, off with you to bed."

But ever-bold Kitty posed a dare. "Go on upstairs to your room. See how long you can stay awake, then you can be up as long as you like." My mother amazingly agreed. Suddenly I was cut adrift from the murmurs and chatter. I wandered off to the upstairs of the big house.

At five it was an enormous privilege to be told I never have to go to sleep, that I might stay up all night if I wanted. Of course the struggle was to stay awake. I had been given a bedroom at the top of the stairs. Needle-thin with slanting ceilings and a window overlooking the driveway, it was seldom used until a month or so before the wedding, when it had been taken over by the local seamstress to assemble the clothes she had been churning out for the bride's trousseau. Upright bolts of shiny, stiff material gleamed in dark corners. Limp dresses still threaded with pins were draped across the one armchair. Gusty had even crept in to stash unopened wedding presents under the bed. Rigid with desire and fatigue, I knelt on the scratchy carpet, trying to distinguish the animals in the faded Oriental pattern, my back pressed against the daybed.

Safe in this makeshift space, I clutched my newest doll, which was dressed exactly as the bride would be, a birthday present from my mother and conjured up by the dressmaker with the same silk she had used for Gusty's dress, adding the same tiny lace collar, even the same miniature pearl necklace. I turned my doll, my friend, over and over. I felt this was perfection. This was all I ever will want, I thought, to be so impeccably dressed, so immaculate, above all to be a bride, to be a grown-up, never to have to go to bed.

—◆—

Gusty's story, her moment of spectacle, captured us all but it was only one more instance of the aunts, their comings and goings, dominating the household. The war was over, but this was still a house of women without men. Every time an airplane droned overhead we would run outside, throw back our heads to the sky. Would it dip its wings to us? "Maybe it's Temple," we cried, hoping for our dashing cousin who had been an air force pilot. It seemed to take a long time for any of these men to come home, to actually extricate themselves from their unit, their uniform, their glory. My own father was somewhere in the Pacific, my mother's only brother still in Europe, and if they weren't dead like my grandfather, or "overseas" as we had been taught to say, the other men in our family were persona non grata.

Two charming uncles had been stricken from the family lists and would not be coming to this weekend celebration. Both Betsy and Theo were undergoing divorces and they spent a lot of time on the telephone, tucked in hideaway corners or weeping on my grandmother's big, white-painted bed. Aunt Betsy had been left by Uncle Stephen, a painter and a womanizer.

On the other hand, Aunt Theo was leaving her husband, Uncle Chauncy. He was much older than she. When he first saw Aunt Theo she was only nineteen but so striking with her Roman nose, white skin and black hair, he knew he had to have her like the paintings and sculpture he collected. Family lore says he fired off a barrage of presents, not just flowers but trees, not just letters but daily beseeching telegrams, until she relented. Uncle Chauncy was most notable in my mind because he was rich, sensationally, exorbitantly rich.

Thus, these were the men in my life, but they were conspicuous by their absence. In fact the only active, possibly present men I had in my lexicon were Santa Claus and Jesus Christ. And over that important weekend of Gusty's wedding, they both were coming. Christmas had been added to the excitement of the wedding. I had absorbed the malarkey about being good for Santa, who didn't really interest me. I was always boringly good, but the idea of presents definitely did interest me.

Somehow I had Santa Claus mixed up in my mind with Jesus. I can't quite figure out how this happened. My family was only conventionally religious, we went to church irregularly and though I had been taught to say the Lord's Prayer, also "Jesus, Tender Shepherd, Hear Me," kneeling, no less, by my bed at night, I was more used to hearing Jesus' name taken in vain. "Jesus!" shouted my father when he was irritated, and when he said "Hell's bells" he laughed.

But Jesus lurked unseen around us. Once I had seen a picture of Jesus in shepherd's robes with a stringy beard and mooning eyes. It must have been the beard that linked Santa Claus and Jesus, those two iconic saviours in my simple mind. They were remote, awesome figures yet they insisted on pushing in on our humdrum routine. I did not want to meet either of them; I was afraid of them. Then suddenly on that night before Gusty's wedding, when I was alone in the stuffy room, engulfed by wedding paraphernalia and dizzy with impending sleep, I was convinced I heard one of them lumbering up the stairs of my grandmother's house.

I was not presumptuous enough to think they both were coming, but the heavy treads I heard outside my door evoked someone of power and authority, someone male, someone who was seeking me. I dove under the tent of bed clothes facedown so that I was completely hidden, jamming my head against the footboard. Hot, stifling, rigid with fear as I listened to ominous thumps and creaks, I imagined someone with boots, maybe the riding boots that I had seen in the entry hall, tall, shiny brown, braced with wooden trees to maintain their imposing fit. Holding my breath, I heard the muffled sound brush by my door and then continue down the hall. Still I did not dare to pull my head up from the heavy load of covers and, still entombed, I finally allowed myself to fall asleep.

In the morning my mother clucked, "You might have been asphyxiated." Someone was making a lot of noise, I insisted, but I was too ashamed to admit who I thought it was.

"Temple arrived last night," she explained, expecting me to be pleased that this golden-god Morgan cousin was now here amongst us for the wedding. I felt a certain delight but also distress. Temple—alluring as he was—was a disturbance. The perfect female harmony had been disrupted. The male presence was as threatening as Jesus' imprecations to impossible saintliness or Santa's phony joviality.

My mother and my aunts became different people when men were around. Aunt Betsy cried on the telephone when Uncle Stephen called to inquire about his daughters; she arrived at tea with her head down, red eyes in a pale face. At the same time I heard Aunt Theo whispering to my mother, "Chauncy has sent butter from his farm, it's a bribe to Mother." Part of me had found Uncle Chauncy charming, and to have real butter, creamy yellow instead of oleo-orange, was a treat. But I resented the way he made Aunt Theo stiffen when he appeared out of the blue, spinning into the driveway with his fancy car, bearing gifts for the entire household; her large dark eyes became grave and stern. "No, Chauncy, I am not coming back to you," was apparently what she said repeatedly, no matter how many emerald brooches or gardenia trees he vainly sent to woo her.

When my mother would talk of her father's sudden death and how she and her sisters with their mother had kept vigil around his body for a whole long night before it was carried away from the sorrowing household, I was half-impressed, half-appalled. Clearly they had worshipped their father, but I had a hard time imagining my levelheaded mother giving in to such grief. I saw them as in thrall to the male presence. They were like the grave figures in a Greek frieze, forever frozen in homage to the dead male.

On their own the Jay sisters were clever, independent women. Aunt Betsy had published her journal of her early married years living on an island off the coast of Maine; *On Gilbert Head* became a best seller and is still well regarded. Aunt Theo worked faithfully at the Arts Students League, Gusty had been a nurse throughout the war. They were athletes, riders and tennis players, they loved parties and dressing up. Yet when I look back at family photographs, they all wear the same controlled smile. They are smiling because they have been told to. They have been so carefully taught to listen, to defer, to appear pleasant and gracious at whatever cost. They stand in the photographs, their heads down, their eyes veiled. They are trapped, not unhappily, but unknowingly, in their culture; their roles, their beauty itself, obediently ready to spring into service.

Little did I know how easy it was to fall into that thralldom, to step unthinkingly into that frieze.

Gusty's wedding captured me in just such a pose.

The marriage ceremony took place on the grounds of Wheatly, the name of the McKim and Meade house where Gran had grown up. There was a small stone chapel that had been built as part of the estate at the end of the nineteenth century, when

Gusty's wedding, 1945

it was common for local gentry to have their own everything—their own railroad car, their own schoolroom—why not their own chapel?

Afterwards everyone came back to my grandmother's for tea, or a sip of champagne and a lot of booze. There must have been something to eat: sliver-thin sandwiches, ham, chicken or watercress, plates of shortbread. I know for sure there was a cake because I have a photograph of myself with my cousins pressed around the bride and groom as they sat side by side at the familiar tea table, now splendidly draped in white damask, everyone smiling achingly widely at the white-sugar-glazed, three-tiered cake. No one is looking at anyone. We are all looking hard at the cake as though it were an adored new baby, ready to enter the family.

I have jammed myself so close up against Gusty in her finery that I wonder how she could even have lifted her arm to hold onto her groom, resplendent in his navy uniform with gold braid, his dark hair slicked back from his beaming face. "Huffy" we called him, breaking into giggles when my grandmother spoke quickly and muffed the names, "Husty and Guffy," she stuttered.

How could Gusty have found time to kiss him, to whisper in his ear? She couldn't; Sybil and Vicky and my other cousin Stephanie and I never left them alone for a minute. They were our dolls come alive, our hero and heroine, the prince and princess poised to bless these little girls in party dresses of pale green wool.

When my great-aunt Kassie sighted us, these four well-scrubbed, well-tended little girls, she sighed and cooed, "Just think of all the men these girls will make happy."

To make men happy—I was already beginning to perceive my purpose in life. Yet there is another picture of myself at this wedding that I had long forgotten. It shows my mother and her vivacious sister-in-law, Trudy Jay, smiling in the privacy of a family joke. Sybil and I stand squarely in front of her. We are joined by my cousin Peter Augustus Jay, my exact twin, born on the same November day (except of course that his birth is far more important than mine as he is the only son of the only son, so now the Jay family name will go on). Pete is dressed in gray flannel shorts with matching Eton-cut jacket. He leans solemnly toward

At the reception, 1945

me. I am another somber figure staring out immobile, looking resignedly at the camera. He is kissing me on the cheek and I am terrified, I am thinking that I must stay perfectly still and soon this embarrassment will be over. Sybil stands alone, apart, abstracted. Is she disgusted with me?

Sybil and I have not always been so standoffish with Pete. He was our friend and neighbor when we came to visit our grandmother. He was an only child and eager for friends and companionship. We were more than friendly; we adored him. Pete was at ease with animals—his mother raised corgis, his father took him horseback riding. When we ran through the woods that separated his parents' house from my grandmother's, he flipped out his perfect fat little pink sausage of a penis and shot a remarkable stream into the mossy trees.

Now he is kissing me and I am terrified. Of what? That we will be discovered? That I love him too much to speak? I have fallen into the male thralldom at the age of five.

Walking between houses with cousin Pete, c. 1945

Least Said, Soonest Mended

SOMETHING WAS MISSING in my growing up—perplexingly missing. It was like the parlor game we played as children. My mother, tray in hand, would circle slowly around the living room, selecting objects from familiar settings: the stamp box off the desk, the green china egg whose top lifted off but had to be placed back just so, maybe a pocket comb because someone was always combing her hair. As soon as the tray was set with a dozen or so objects, she would place it before us children. We sat silently for a few minutes, absorbing this small icon of household memorabilia. Then swiftly she lifted it away, out of sight. We would scurry for pen and paper to list the contents of the absent tray. Something was always missing from my list, and something was missing from my growing up.

Just what it was, was difficult to pinpoint. I had every accoutrement my school reading primer said one should have. My parents loved us. My grandmother Jay remained a bright, beckoning source of solace and warmth. My aunts with their families flocked round at holiday time and during summer vacations. Our house was our own, with a backyard and a car in the garage. There was even a dog for a while. In first grade we read, "Come Dick. Come and see. Come, come. Come and see Spot." But for me the story was not complete. I flipped to the back of the reader for more interesting words and more intriguing situations. Words like "accident" or "argument," anything that might hint at what was beneath the surface. But these words were never mentioned and I would have to force my attention back to Dick and Spot.

We lived in Cambridge, Massachusetts, on a quiet side street called Larch Road, just off the main thoroughfare of Brattle Street. My parents had moved there at the end of World War II, when my father decided he could not bear to go back to the confines of Wall Street corporate law. Happy at Harvard from his undergraduate days in the late 1920s, he decided to ally himself with the great rush of young veterans who were returning to the college to finish their education. In the fall of 1945 he turned his back on the comfortable privileges of both my parents' New York City heritage and moved up the coast to this bastion of academia. My father was a member of Bill Bender's admissions committee at Harvard, the group that sought out so many young men coming home from war, seeking a place in the new order of things. My father's role was to make life easier for their re-entry, their return to the "normal."

With his benignly nonchalant and witty approach to student life, Frankie Kinnicutt, age forty by 1948, was a success at his job. But nothing was easy in our gray-shuttered house. There

Our house at 15 Larch Road with Tizzy, Cambridge, 1946

was, in fact, a distinct dis-ease between my mother and my father. In typically muted, well-bred fashion, nothing dramatic or violent ever happened. Occasionally voices were raised and doors slammed, but it was more what was not said, and what was not done. My parents did not touch each other. They barely looked each other in the eye. My sisters and I watched and listened, though we never said anything, particularly to each other. Our parents seemed to meet only in their comings and goings: my

FPK with his daughters, 1947

mother returning from errands, her hair "done" in a stiff little helmet; my father leaving, his head down, pulling on his overcoat, in a hurry to get out without speaking. I would lie awake at night wondering why my mother who was so good, and so constant, was less interesting, less exciting than my father who was so unreliable, so upsetting.

To grow up in Cambridge was to be ever conscious of the river, the Charles, which wove its way from the countryside along the edge of the city. We took picnics to its banks, watched crew races, and, as schoolgirls, trudged past the river every day on our way home from school. Lugging book bags with sweaters tied around our waists, we threw sticks from the arch of the Eliot Bridge, then ran to the other side to watch them float lazily by. In spring on Coolidge Hill the Charles flooded the marshy streams of our school's fields. Willows grew by the lower depths. There we sat at recess-time, twisting branches into wands or whips, depending on the game. In winter the river sometimes froze. We held our breath as intrepid college students tested the ice with their overshoes flapping at their ankles. I knew I would never be allowed to skate on the dangerous, tempting river. I think about the Charles and I think about my mother. Do they remind me of each other, running silent and constant through my life?

When we were sick my mother threw herself with an almost passionate intensity into our small worlds of flus and fevers. I lay in bed, listening to her quick, firm tread, as she ran up and down the narrow staircase, bringing trays, basins, potties, doctors' messages. Her step on the stairs seemed determined to stamp out the malady, however minor. Shaking the thermometer seemed to take a long time; she peered at the heavy bar of slithering silver, anxiously waiting for it to float to the fragile mark that meant safe, normal, no more worry. Once she shook the thermometer so vigorously it snapped in two. I watched as the sinuous liquid instantaneously dissolved. If my mother was the powerful river permanently embedded in our lives, my father was that shimmering, evanescent mercury, disappearing before you knew it.

This sense of dis-ease wafted around me like the warm air blowing up the flat floor registers we used to heat the house during long New England winters. We sisters stood over the grates to let air blow up under our skirts, to make them bell out around us like ladies in old-fashioned picture books. I wanted to be one of those careful, perfect ladies with their fans and parasols. But instead I was stuck, trapped in a house with the sad air of unhappiness blowing through it. It was a fact of life, like struggling early out of bed on dark mornings, laboring over homework at night. There was nothing to do but endure. The unhappiness in our house had to be borne as a secret.

I was interested in secrets. They seemed to offer a solution to what was missing. And so it was that growing up, the gravest infraction I ever committed was to read my parents' diaries. I must have been around ten. In a way, I suppose these notebooks were maps, because I needed direction. I was determined to ferret out secrets about my parents. I wanted to figure out what was going on in their heads. It was not that they presented themselves as so powerful and all-knowing. I was fully aware of their shortcomings. It was just that they seemed absent, even when they were most acutely present. Driving us to school, eating meals together, even on long summer days of vacation, I did not feel they were really there. The fact that they both kept diaries must mean, I reasoned, that they had things to hide.

My mother's diary was a small, neatly bound book of polished brown calf, butter-smooth to the touch. There was a clasp for some tiny key, but she innocently never kept it locked. It sat on a lower shelf on her bedside table. On winter afternoons when others were out at piano lessons or dentist appointments, I would slip the diary out of its cranny and settle down on the faded rose-colored rug, my back nestling against the mattress-ticking dust ruffle to read once again the well-known pages. To actually sit on the bed itself would have been too much an invasion of privacy.

This was the diary my mother had kept as a young mother and wife, in Florida during the World War II. She was far away from home. This book was a record of her new, foreign life. It is not the kind of journal my mother would have bought for herself. She had obviously been given it and she clearly felt bound to fill its gilt-edged vellum pages. The entries were not interesting: "children have chicken pox," "Bushes for dinner; they bring lobster," "Camilla is engaged."

Sometimes even my mother would herself read us passages from the diary, but they were always the same, flat impersonal lines that told me nothing.

Still, there was something that led me to continue, seeking out this diary as a repository of clues to my self-effacing mother. I wanted her to have a secret (clearly my father had them), so I invented one for her. Or was it for myself? I had come across the line, "Mom calls to tell me Henry Atherton killed at Guadalcanal." It was the starkest, most interesting reference in the whole relentlessly dry journal. We all knew what Guadalcanal was: cousin Eddie Morgan had been trapped there on that godforsaken Pacific island for months. I even knew who Henry Atherton was. There was a picture of him in her old day-school yearbook my mother unearthed for us when we were home sick from school. He squinted out at me, stocky, serious at nine years old. "I never knew him very well," my mother insisted. "He went away early to boarding school; his parents were friends of Mom and Dad's." Still, I savored the image of Henry Atherton. I hugged the memory of him to myself. Which was more compelling, more mysterious—that he was so gravely handsome or that he was dead?

My father's diary was a different matter. His I came upon by accident, unlike my mother's; she was practically begging her daughters to tell her she was just as prudent and unruffled as she appeared in those impassive pages. I was playing hide-and-seek on a rainy day upstairs on the third floor. I crammed myself into the dusty back closet, the one where suitcases and extra empty boxes were kept. The eaves were too good a hiding place. No one could find me. I could hear the voices of the players drift away but rather than rejoin the group, I began rummaging around amongst the boxes that no one would use but could not bear to throw away. I came upon an old striped dress box marked with a clear hand I knew well: "F.P.K., letters and journals." Even now those initials have a visceral power over me. I knew with deep, stomach-pit sureness that I was breaking a terrible cardinal rule of privacy, but I pressed ahead excitedly. Here at last were some instructions for discovering my father, even though he lived right down the hall, even though I would probably sit at table with him that night.

My mother wrote with the fading mark of a pencil. My father wrote with a fountain pen, in dark ink that raced across the pages of a floppy schoolboy notebook. Evidently this journal was written at the time of his engagement to my mother in 1937. Apparently she had asked him to keep a record of what he was thinking at this momentous time. There was a lot about what he was reading—Henry Green, Max Beerbohm, Ernest Hemingway, but I flipped past those names. I was looking for concrete facts, not just musings and opinions. Suddenly I was pierced through. The line flashed up at me. "Up late talking to Theo, S. very cross." Theo of course was my mother's younger sister; S. of course was my mother, Sybil. A few lines later I read, "I love looking at naked women." A little fright clutched my heart. Now I knew I was treading in murky waters. I hurried away, too startled to continue.

I had forgotten to even replace the lid of the box or turn off the light. It was still blazing away when my mother went upstairs to retrieve one of those rejected cartons. I had never seen her as icy and forbidding as when she came to speak to me that night, alone in my bedroom with the door shut. After I had finished hearing about privacy and respect—all those rules I knew and yet also knew at the same time I would break again and again—she said to me, "If there's something you want to know, you should just ask me." Then we looked at each other in surprise because we both knew that was impossible.

—⁂—

Open communication was rare in our family. We preferred to lose ourselves in other people's stories or in tales of other families through the enlivening realm of books. The prevailing mantra was my grandmother's dictum: "Least said, soonest mended."

At least my mother could turn her muteness to advantage.

In our family, she was the listener. Just as she had sat by the phone so quietly, so patiently that day in Florida when I whacked off my hair, she was forever listening to someone in trouble, in pain, or who just wanted to let off steam. At home her post was a particular sofa in the back living room. "The sitting room," as my mother called it, was aptly named, as that was the one space in which, on occasion, she did actually sit.

In the morning, after the flurry of our leave-taking for school was over, she permitted herself a rest on the low-slung sofa by the window with her post-breakfast cup of coffee and the crossword puzzle. There she sat, warmed by the trickle of eastern

My mother and her daughters, 1948

sunlight. In the evening, she shifted her seat to the other end of the sofa where she was near the lamp, backed by a wall of beloved books.

But first in the evening, she fed her young daughters suppers of minute steaks and frozen French fries at the kitchen table (because we were not invited to eat in the dining room with our parents until we were twelve). She then washed up the dishes. (Paid a penny a plate, we helped dry the dishes during Lent so that we could put the money in our church's mite boxes.) That task over, my mother hurried upstairs, changed into not-quite evening clothes, but something long and soft, and had a drink in the sitting room with my father. They both cared about their cocktail, he for relaxation, she for fortitude. She then returned to the kitchen to make an adult supper—roast chicken and again frozen, never fresh, peas, but with soup as a first course and cut-up fruit for dessert. She sat at the dining room table with my father, carried the dishes back out to the kitchen, washed up again, finally permitting herself a retreat to her favorite spot in the sitting room to sip a beer by herself. There I would come to curl up beside her, to tell her, in exquisitely exciting detail, to me, about school, to read my composition over, to check a math problem. Sometimes at that perch she read aloud to us; sometimes slowly, lingeringly we leafed through family photograph albums. I certainly never asked her what she had been doing. The sofa seemed similar to my mother—discreet, unpretentious, but of a certain style and important to the room.

The second living room was around the corner from the larger reception room where my mother sat upright at her narrow secretary desk to pay bills, and where my father installed a bulky box of a radio and on top of that a gramophone because he was the one who lay on the sofa and listened to his collection of records, anything from Beethoven to Rodgers and Hammerstein. This was a space as near as any that was shared, and neutral. Here was a neat paradigm of how my parents conducted their lives— my father so alive with music and gaiety, my mother so intent upon order and thrift.

There was one time when my mother did give in to music and gaiety. One evening that boxy radio began to play the seductive tune of Cole Porter's "Night and Day."

"Oh," cried my mother, "the song of my youth." Her face lit up, she reached out almost instinctively for a partner. Who was there but me on a Sunday night, tweaking the dial, hoping to find my favorite Jack Benny program.

"Let's dance," she said and I thought she was teasing.

"I don't know how," I protested, a little alarmed at my mother's vivacity.

"I will teach you," she insisted, circling my waist with her arm, lifting up my right hand in a firm clasp. "This is called the box step, it's easy."

And so we glided, however hesitantly, through the front living room, out into the hall with the radiator blowing its familiar, uneven puff of dusty air.

"Careful, don't trip," said my mother as she deftly guided me around the grate. "Come on, darling, the important thing is to relax and follow your partner. You must do just what he does and always, always, follow his lead."

Thus was my first dancing lesson, and it never occurred to me that it was odd that it should come not from my fun-loving father but from my cautious mother.

When my mother did talk about herself was on the nights I was allowed to sleep in her bed, the big double bed my parents surprisingly shared with a hump in the middle. That hump said everything to me about their marriage—more than watching them in the hall averting each other's eye, more than hearing their irritated voices hiss at night behind the closed bedroom door. But sleeping with my mother on the odd night when my father disappeared (literally, since I was not quite sure just where he was—off to New York on the train, away duck-hunting with friends, fled from the face of the earth?) served as a kind of balm, a return to innocence.

On those nights my mother became my friend, relaxed and spontaneous. We chattered on in the dark. One of our favorite games was following the thread of our conversation. "How did we ever get started on this?" we asked each other when we ended up in some surprising place in our meandering. I was never tired of stories of herself as a child. I didn't want to hear any tale of how she felt inept or insecure at school. I sought not parallels with myself, but differences. I wanted to hear how happy she was, adored by her parents who incidentally adored each other. Her father took her horseback riding, even hunting on early cold mornings. Her grandparents gave her a dance on her eighteenth birthday, but because it was the Depression, the invitation read, "small dance." It was a fairy-tale life and I could never grasp her fall from grace.

There was nothing to say, really. My parents had drifted apart amidst the usual stumbling blocks of marriage. He liked to spend money, she insisted on watching every penny. He liked to shine, she preferred to hide. There were his idle flirtations. He needed lots of attention. So did she, but she kept herself tight-lipped and undemanding. He avoided grown up responsibilities, so she walled herself up in an impregnable fortress, and there I was in her bed, with the hump in the middle.

Quatre Diables

ON HIS BEDSIDE TABLE, my father kept a cracked ceramic ash-tray. It was white with a fluted edge; inscribed in its center was the French proverb,

Trois filles
et une mère;
Quatre diables
pour le père.

The doggerel stuck with me. Here was a vision of a man be-witched by his naughty, charming wife and their three daugh-ters. Is this the way our father wanted us to be, an equal match for his outrageousness?

—ᴍ—

Three sisters we were and, though hardly devilish, we did maintain a firm hand in the balance of power of family life.

FPK with his new Minox camera, 1955

Everything in family life mattered to Sybil and Tizzy. Whose turn it was to set the table, where my parents were going for dinner, who would be left in charge of us, this feverish trio?

Sybil, two years older than I, and Tizzy, four years younger, met and matched with equal fervor in their intense desire to be heard, to be noticed in the family hierarchy. I was caught in between, straining to catch their drift of just why all the fuss was so important. Often I longed to wiggle away from the ferocity of their caring. Yet as sisters we were attached, almost symbiotically, in our intimacy. We shared clothes, tickled each other's arms, checked each other's breath for sweetness, brushed each other's hair. Even now, many years later, in thinking about those childhood years, I realize I cannot extricate myself from the "we." "We felt, we played, we knew." Where was the "I"?

My sisters formed an alliance from which I could never quite separate myself. With my sisters I felt safe, linked together in a curious alchemy of early instinctive loyalty and later deep, satisfying intimacy.

I was like the Chinese porcelain statue in Gran Jay's collection of oddments. Fashioned in the image of a Mandarin figure, dressed in the finery of silk robes and embroidered pantaloons, smooth-faced yet balding, it sat cross-legged, with small hands resting on its knees. When you touched the top of its head, it nodded, a slight, imperceptible nod of assent. If you continued to pat its head, it continued to nod. If no one bothered to touch the figure, it sat impassive, immobile. I felt this way with my sisters—fascinated, mute, observing. I was trapped by my obsession to please, so eager to please that I was unable to act, to speak, to stand up for myself.

Sybil and Tizzy closed around me, lovingly, enthusiastically, certainly not to hurt me, but to claim me. They wanted me on their side, in whatever battle they were waging, whether it was with our parents about bedtime or with the neighborhood girls' clique as to who should star in our next play. Now I realize they merely wanted me to strike out on my own, but since I could not quite master that trick of living, they proceeded to do it for me.

My sisters lived in permanent states of defiance to my parents, to the school authorities, to the world in general. They typified what my parents called the attitude of "agin" the government. When "everyone knew" in 1948 that Thomas Dewey was going to be president, Sybil, age ten, hung on for Truman. She sometimes took my breath away when she talked back to my essentially benign—if somewhat distracted—parents. It was not out of any ill feeling. Sybil just had an irrepressible urge to be in the right. Once at school she organized a petition to demonstrate to my parents that no one went to bed as early as we did. Yet she was also known to burst into my bedroom at night where I lay in the dark, listening on the radio to the muffled sounds of *The Great Gildersleeve*. "How dare you!" she'd hiss triumphantly. "You know we're not allowed to be up this late." Conversely, she suffered from ferocious migraines, and we all learned to tiptoe around the house when she was struck.

Her release from her acts of defiance was in make-believe. Sybil wanted to be an actress. Her bedroom was an Aladdin's den of movie magazines, theater programs and love comics. She had her own radio as we all did but as a teenager she went one daring step further and saved her babysitting money to buy a television set, which she then hid in her closet. Television was considered trash by my old-guard parents. Popular culture was something that never crossed their path, but gradually they both would trickle in to Sybil's bedroom to watch *Playhouse 90* and our favorite, *I Love Lucy*.

Sybil, ever the performer, dressed herself in alarmingly exotic ways. Spindle-thin, she piled springy net crinolines under

Maisie and Sybil, 1955

bright circular skirts, cinched her tiny waist in broad elastic belts and flounced off to school in worn ballet slippers, ignoring my mother's manifestos on sturdy lace-up oxfords. In the afternoons after school she directed plays in our backyard with neighborhood friends. Actually they were closer to soap operas, complete with commercials. I was allowed to sing, "Sudsy Dudsy is so fine; makes your clothes just plain shine," words and music by Sybil, of course.

Bossy as she was, everyone gravitated to her. She was the classic oldest child, eager for control, anxious of displacement, but with a bursting, loving heart. Her school friends flocked around her, trusting her to solve their romances, loan them a charm bracelet, advise them on how to handle their parents. Even the faculty fell under her spell. Sybil was too wrapped up in her own make-believe world ever to be a really diligent student, but her teachers indulged her, finishing her onerously difficult bookbinding project for her and letting her skip out early from afternoon sports.

I was proud to be her sister, an accolade she tried to shrug off. Getting dressed in the morning, I would hang over the banister, watching to see what she was wearing. Still in my pajamas, I would then try to approximate her dash and glamour. Sybil would catch one look at me, her pallid double, and race back upstairs. "I will not have Maisie copying me," she'd announce to my placating mother.

Tizzy, christened Elizabeth and younger than Sybil by six years, used silence as her weapon against our parents as much as Sybil used commands. A sleek little cat, she reigned from her third-floor aerie—attic rooms that were the largest in the house. Tizzy seemed to get her own way with my parents because they both felt guilty about her existence. She had been born toward the end of the war as my father was already drifting out of the marriage. My mother would feed her third-born, another disappointing daughter, as tears slid down her cheeks, mixing with the cereal.

My father wooed Tizzy as his *bonne poupée*. Certainly not eager

Tizzy in her attic room, 1955

to be cast as the "good little doll," Tizzy stonily refused his advances, due to the very fact that he ignored our mother. She cast herself as my mother's protector, snapping at my father at the slightest pretext. The more perverse she was, the more he persisted. Like a spurned Lothario, he never stopped courting her, even naming his dinghy *Tiz*.

Even my usually evenhanded mother spoiled her, installing a special pink Princess telephone in her bedroom. Secretive and sexy, Tizzy had boyfriends with whom she smoked and French-kissed. She wore green eye shadow and tight sheath skirts to school.

Tiz knew how to take chances. One night when she was about eleven, she snuck into the second-floor guest room where two college girls were spending the night on a visit to their Harvard beaux. Larch Road was considered a suitable perch for these daughters of family friends who were journeying to Cambridge for rambunctious football weekends.

We sisters stood in awe of these young women. We envied their glossy pageboys swinging back from smooth cheeks. We stared as they edged red lipstick around pouty mouths and listened to them giggle as my father offered them Dubonnet on the rocks in the living room while they waited for their young men.

But on this particular night these two girls had left early, their high heels clattering down the front steps. Tiz crept into the guest room and began to rummage through their suitcases. We knew nothing of this escapade; for once, we were a quiet family engaged in our own quiet pursuits, Mummy curled up with the crossword puzzle, my father dozing with a book. Tizzy burst into our midst, barefoot, in "borrowed" loose cardigan and pearls. Below her waist she had pulled on one girl's lacy pink girdle. And down this fancy front, she had jammed a heart-shaped, black velvet shoe tree, the kind of firm stuffing women used in those days to keep the taper of their shoe in perfect party shape. Tiz had wedged this little cushion down the pale transparent lace of the girdle, down to her crotch so that it appeared she had now sprouted a dark thatch of pubic hair.

She danced about the living room, a pixie hoyden, half intoxicated with herself, half embarrassed by her own daring. My parents stared, silent and slack-jawed. I cowered behind Sybil. What kind of trouble had Tizzy gotten herself into now?

But suddenly the silence broke. My mother giggled, my father laughed as he said proudly, "Jesus, Tiz, what a card you are!"

I was not jealous of this, or any, parental attention. Like everyone else I wanted to makeup for some ancient, unspoken wound. In her third-floor lair, we played with abandon, dressing up in my mother's discarded evening clothes and overturning furniture to create caves and palaces. I spun out such sad stories to entertain her that we both ended up in tears, a pastime we both relished. But then I also felt compelled to scuttle back downstairs. I had enjoyed myself too much. I needed to reinstate myself in the calming world of homework, duty, churning out flawless academic papers, washing my hands again and again.

Thus I cautiously wended my way in this uneasy family. It never occurred to me to rebel on my own—there was too much of that going on already. If my sisters advanced, I retreated. If they were bright birds of prey, I was an ostrich, sticking my head in the sand. I was captivated by my sisters. I admired their spirit and spunk as much as I wanted to avoid disturbing the peace myself. Still, they caused too much trouble and trouble was something I wanted to avoid—until much, much later.

The one indulgence I permitted myself was the concoction of elaborate fantasies. In those airy worlds anything was possible. I only wanted to escape, to reorder, to tidy up, to rearrange any displeasing facts of my surroundings. Sybil and I invented two imaginary families, the Chapins and the Gingers. All the facts and bits and pieces of our lives—pleasant and unpleasant—were woven into the lives of the Chapins and the Gingers, transmuted into smiling fairy stories.

Sybil was in charge of the Ginger family, which consisted of the parents, two daughters, both named Virginia, and an elusive, androgynous son named Dordup. This oddly named son showed high originality on her part. I just took the name of my second-grade teacher, pert Mrs. Chapin, and gave her a burgeoning family of at least six or seven kids, all of whom had the names of my parents' friends' children, "Hunty, Phippy and Cotty." (Also, of course a girl like me, "Maisie," and her brave, bold twin, "Ricky.")

Telling tales of these imaginary families to each other, we rocked back and forth in straight-back kitchen chairs we had dragged out on the icy little back porch. We leaned forward correcting each other, like two old ladies chatting away the afternoon. We took a piece of news from some stray fact we had gleaned from our mother's casual remarks about the events of her little world. Once, she told us a son of a friend had fallen and was in the hospital. We seized on this scrap of drama, making up a whole new richer, more lurid story. We knit the tale together, passing essential details back and forth. "He broke his leg … no, his arm." "No, he cracked his skull open," said Sybil, warming to the subject.

Surprises, even violence, excited Sybil. It appealed to her literary sense of mystery and intrigue, while I only wanted everyone to end up rich and happy.

When Sybil was not around to confabulate with, I talked to myself.

"Hoogily-Boogily" I called it. I sat in my room by myself and spun stories out loud about the people I knew or wished I knew. Again I shuffled the facts of family life just as I played solitaire with a worn deck of cards or straightened and re straightened the ornaments on the curly-maple bookshelf in my bedroom. In

At home with a book, 1955

Hoogily-Boogily, no one ever shouted or sulked. Life "there" was a kind of perpetual birthday party with lots of presents and fancy dresses, except that when the party was over, no one ever got headaches or threw up from too much cake. Even in reality, I never ate too much cake.

I was able to concoct such stories because I was in the grip of my addiction: reading.

Growing up as a Geiger counter, alert to beneath-the-surface problems, I found reading a solace. I read all the time, early, late, in bed, in the bathroom, sometimes even under the bed hiding "dirty pictures" from my mother. I read at school, coming home from school, before supper, after supper. My mother sometimes had to curtail my reading. "You haven't been outside all day. You must have a breath of fresh air," she would insist, and I would stand motionless on the front porch, dumbly waiting to be released back to my book. My mother herself always had a book at hand and read aloud to us sisters. She had a lovely low voice and she liked to read aloud. I was drawn to anything my mother liked to do. She so rarely permitted herself pleasure, but she read from the books she remembered as a child: *Peter Pan*, *The Wind in the Willows*, anything by A.A. Milne. These tales featuring animals were a bit far-fetched for me. I needed to be firmly grounded with people in the complexities of daily life.

What I read was not lofty: the Bobbsey Twins; the chatty works of a Mrs. Fletcher; which were based on stories of twins around the world; all the prairie tales of Laura Ingalls Wilder; and a wonderful growing-up, coming-of-age series by Maud Hart Lovelace about three inseparable friends called Betsy, Tacy and Tib, who lived in Minnesota in a serene faraway town called Deep Valley.

I was drawn to stories of twins because I imagined as a twin you experienced total intimacy and loyalty; you were irrefutably chosen by one special person, you were thus forever safe. I also liked books that were part of a series. Perhaps it was that sense of sameness and familiarity, of never wanting to believe you could lose these friends and companions you had made and loved and wept over.

Happily, Sybil read all the same books, so we were forever exchanging notes and gushing confidences about these people who were so real to us. We minded that Tacy's baby sister died of scarlet fever, but we cheered up when Pa Wilder made it back through the storm with the flour and the firewood during the terrible winter of '87 or when Betsy took a night train all by herself to visit Tib in Milwaukee. Sybil read other, much racier stories that I never quite had the stomach for. She even crossed the line and got into boys' books like *Treasure Island* and *Captains Courageous* but I hung back; I wasn't interested in adventure unless it was of the heart. Of course we were both infatuated with movie magazines. There again Sybil took the lead. She saved her allowance for *Photoplay* and *Silver Screen* and then I, the penny-pincher, hung around her bedroom and scooped up the ones she discarded. We were scrupulous in our devotion to Elizabeth Taylor and have followed the successive line of her husbands to this day.

But our all-time favorite book, the one we really knew by heart and could recite to each other chapter and verse, was *Little Women*. How could this tale of sisters who loved dress-up and make-believe with the steadfast, goody-goody mother and the venerated, absent father miss with us? And Louisa May (May was my name too, I was proud to note) Alcott was practically a neighbor! The Alcott family house still stood in Concord, Massachusetts. It was a mere half an hour from our faded grey frame house to their faded grey frame house. My greatest treat was visiting this house with our mother on slushy Sunday afternoons, when Sybil and I would argue over which room it was where John had proposed to Meg and just where it was that Beth had died. I once tried to trick her into believing I had seen one of Jo's discarded apple cores in the dusty attic but she responded by telling me I was as stuck-up as Amy.

Jo was important to us growing up. In my heart of hearts I had to admit I was most like Meg in my desire for the niceties of life, for pretty clothes and harmonious family relations. When Meg magnanimously lends scruffy Jo one of her gloves to hold decorously (and hide the stain on her dress) at their first grown-up party, I ached for her generosity and shared her pique because we both knew Jo would tiresomely lose the one good glove. Meg could hardly wait to marry some nice respectable man and have babies and make jam, which was just what I planned for my future. But Jo sang a siren song in my half-cocked ear. Jo was tall and ungainly, she lost her temper and quarreled with Amy, but Jo was a writer. And she had a man in her life who wasn't just a flirtation or a convenience. He was a friend. Jo held out the possibility of freedom. Jo was full of high spirits and flung her devil-may-care vitality in the face of her pious family but, like me, she was deeply devoted to her mother. But unlike me she also sensed and kept a distance from her mother. Jo understood she and her mother were separate people.

I could never be, never wanted to be, the "devil" Jo March was, but I understood with her the power of being a sister.

My Mother Was the Mirror

ALL THREE OF US tacitly agreed in our role as our mother's protector.

My mother was the mirror I peered into to see myself. This is how I thought I should, could, would be. It was a mirror of silver. Silver in our house hung around as bits and pieces of an inheritance or long-ago wedding presents: candlesticks brought out for dinner parties, a silver tray etched with a hunting scene, a cigar box for my father from the Porcellian Club. Once a maid who was in for an evening party put a silver platter in the oven to warm it for serving; it melted in the heat and my mother bit her lip in fierce vexation. She complained about the silver, about having to polish it all the time, but it still meant something to her.

When you look into a silver plate you see shadows, a marred surface, but there is a glimmer of your own image, or so you feel. With my mother I felt I was neat, clean, tidy, ordered—and in trouble. I wanted to be with her, but in some faint, frightened way, I also wanted not to be her. Her aura of unhappiness was too threatening. I felt responsible for her. I wanted to do something, anything, to make her appear happy. But I was so in the grip of her anxiety I only knew how to mimic her. I revered and adored her and could not be carefree myself because that would be disloyal.

I worshipped my mother, but like most goddesses she was remote, remote in her pain, remote in her goodness. When I was not at school I spent most of the day hovering close to home. Friends were inviting and tempting but peripheral. I tailed my mother closely. What was she doing? Where was she going? When she went away, which was seldom, I would shut myself in her closet and press her limp-hanging clothes to my face in an empty embrace.

Her moments of leisure were rare. Sometimes I would sit with her as she took her bath, just to be near her, to guard her and—as I never could admit to myself—to slyly observe her.

In our house there were two bathrooms for five people. On the second floor was my parents' bathroom. It was meant to be just for them, but Sybil and I managed to scuttle in and out like scrawny water rats, leaving a trail of wet footprints. The other bathroom was on the third floor for Tizzy and whatever keeper might be lodged there.

The so-called grown-ups' bathroom was pale green, the color of murky water, with matching pale green tiles reaching halfway up the wall. The tub and sink were large sculptures of a yellowing ivory color. The tub sunk close into the floor. Lights were in the shape of glass fans nestled against the mirrored cabinet over the broad mouth of the washbasin. High above the tub was the one window of the room. It was covered partially by a leaded screen of colored glass, and behind that was the regular window pane overlooking the back yard.

It was a mysterious grotto of a room, guarding secrets of adulthood. Its furnishings bulked imposingly to me. They were so different from the spare, white, freestanding tub, toilet and sink of the ordered kingdom of the third floor. My parents' bathroom was a bizarre anomaly in our otherwise conventional house. It was a place to luxuriate, yet no one in our family ever indulged themselves because we had to hurry up to let the next person in. The room must have been a thirties escapist fantasy for some previous owner. The toilet seat was covered in a fish-scale pattern formica that was beginning to chip, even as we first arrived.

Once I was allowed into this private space, I would sit on the toilet with the fish-scale lid down while my mother lingered in the great ark of the tub. As usual, nothing was said. I only watched her. Her long body bobbled, weightless in the water. She modestly draped a washcloth over her alarming bush of pubic hair. Her breasts floated upwards, brown nipples dark and soft as pansies. I sat in awkward fascination. She let her head rest on the round shoulder of the tub. When she stretched out her slender length of leg, her toes still did not reach the fat knobs of faucets. The water broke her body into glimmering fragments. She swam away from me, a mermaid, a free spirit, a being not my mother. This moment of bathing was one of the few times I ever saw my mother in repose. Soon she clambered out, grabbing a skimpy towel, scurrying down the narrow hall, on to her

Tizzy and Maisie, c. 1945

next task, her next duty. She used to say she never liked that bathroom. "The first thing I wanted to change was all those silly colors." But she never did. She was reluctant to take on any kind of change. She was more a guardian than an innovator, a mender rather than a builder.

Using our baby sister's bathroom gave Sybil and me permission to behave as children. I invaded Tizzy's space, squeezing myself beside her in the narrow claw-foot tub. We would splash and laugh, screaming when the soapy water stung our eyes, the tub overflowing on the floor. Marion the nurse would shake her head as she mopped up the mess. "You girls are high-sterical." At last I could be naughty, irresponsible.

Light poured into that little space, as the tub sat directly under a wide, square window. One could sit hunched up in the tub, knees akimbo, warmed by the afternoon sun, gazing onto the street below. From my perch I could spot big, rangy Gordon Lund striding home from football practice. I could see him; but he didn't even imagine I was watching him. I shivered in delight in my nudity, drawing my knees even tighter to my bony chest.

In one corner of that bathroom stood an ancient scale my mother had brought with her from her girlhood home. Tall and spindly, the treasured apparatus had a gooseneck rod of a measuring stick that you pulled out of its rusty spine to see how much you had grown that past summer. When I stepped on the platform of the scales, there would be a little tremble, a shudder of anticipation from the scales themselves. They would wait while I fiddled with the heavy chipped disks of metal. I lined them up in a tidy row. First came the big chunks of fifty pounds, then the smaller crescent slivers of ten and twenty. I watched the arrow of the lever hover. Was it better to let it quiver, just slightly brushing the top of the bar? Or was it more satisfying to let it sink with a thud to the bottom mark? I never understood how these cold circles of weight that one could hold in the palm of one's hand could equal one's gangly frame. My body seemed so complicated. How could it be reduced to such simple terms?

Just as my mother slid away from me in the tub, she did not project ease with her body. She had a way of muting herself. Watching her strain forward into the looking glass of her mirror-topped dressing table, I longed for her to emblazon herself with her few modest pieces of jewelry, some perfume and makeup for color and life. But only her mouth arched for an obligatory smear of lipstick. Pressing her fingertips to her freshly reddened lips, she would pat small circles onto her anxious, oval face. This was daring, for we had been taught to give color to our pallor by biting our lips and slapping our cheeks.

The message that filtered down from my mother was "Don't look at me, but tell me I'm pretty." She moved with her head down, her shoulders bent forward, hurrying on to the next task. Yet as I grew older I came to notice a shared preoccupation, however unconscious, amongst my grandmother, my mother and her sisters, with looks. They talked a lot about how people looked and how they presented themselves:

"Wiz is pretty but Kate is the real beauty of the family."
"It's too bad Mittie has let herself go."
"Jessie is plain but she has real chic."

Being sexy was never mentioned. That was not the point. Someone might be considered "fetching," but that usually meant her smile or her hat.

It was important, a highest goal, to be something called "beautiful." It was something we were never supposed to talk about wanting to be, but a state of bliss to which we were to aspire.

There was the body, which was unmentionable, and the message, which was to present yourself as perfect, unsullied, unattainable. The desire for a pleasing aura was one of those things that was never mentioned but whose subtle presence had impact and weight. It started with my grandmother.

My mother and her sisters grew up the shy daughters of a beautiful mother. Gran, with her auburn hair swept in a loose pompadour of curls, and with her hazel eyes and throaty laugh, never gave the impression of caring how she looked. But her daughters worshipped the legend of her beauty. They themselves were known for their long legs, low voices and grave, deep-set eyes. Natural, unaffected Gran was a standard by which we all measured ourselves and our friends and the faces we pored over in our beloved movie magazines. "You girls are much prettier than Elizabeth Taylor," my mother would lamely pronounce. Unlikely we knew, but if so, how would it ever happen?

I was never sure just how I did appear to the outside view. Pretty, plain, unusual, nondescript? Once, at a friend's, we wheeled crazily around, chasing each other through empty rooms. I raced around a corner, bumping into an icy hard wall. Suddenly there was something unfamiliar jumping out, staring wide-eyed at me. I backed away, shaken and confused by the shock of the mirror's leer. "What's the matter, did ya scare yourself?" asked my friend.

As a child I knew I carefully presented myself as inoffensive with regular features, neat and clean with thick brown hair held severely back with ribbons or barrettes from my well-scrubbed face. But I was locked in a prison of self-consciousness. That was

the monster that had frightened me in the mirror. I felt unconnected to my body. Dark flecks of hair blurred my upper lip. My
eyebrows grew straight across my forehead. My legs and arms
were like slightly furry animal limbs.

Years later my husband told me he could pick me out in a
crowd because of the way I walked with my head down. I knew I
was ducking my head to avoid something, that strange, glaring
presence I had once bumped into in the mirror.

Of course, thinking about how one looked was taboo in
Cambridge. There, mothers flopped about in long, limp skirts
and flat shoes, everyone lived in hand-me-downs, and we three
Kinnicutt sisters were teased at birthday parties because we
wore red ballet slippers from Capezio in New York, instead of
the expected-in-Boston black patent leather party shoes.

When my mother would return from her weekly hair appoint-
ment, she ran her fingers through the iron-careful set, "just to
mess it up a bit," she apologized. Yet there were countless slight
references as to who in the family shared Gran's cheekbones,
her turned-up nose, or who in the family tree had the famous
black Jay hair. ("We came from Ireland, shipwrecked in Spain,"
insisted Aunt Betsy.) Once Sybil caught me posturing giddily in
front of the one long mirror in our house. "Maisie's admiring
herself," she rushed, sputtering, to my mother. My mother drew
me aside as though I had committed a major infraction. "Your
looks have nothing to do with you. It's all part of the family
and your eyebrows are just like Aunt Theo's, who inherited them
from my father."

It never occurred to me that my mother was beautiful. She

My mother, c. 1940

projected such unhappiness, how could she be? We sisters tried to protect her, to keep her on some lofty pedestal—particularly on her birthday, the fourth of June.

Behind our house was a dull patch of lawn that had trouble growing under a knotty maple tree. In the backyard, as it was called—because that's what it was, not a garden—were a few forsythia bushes and a forlorn trellis propped under a kitchen window. A hedge of lilac formed the boundaries between us and our neighbors. My mother was not a gardener. She kept an immaculate house where she preferred to remain, only trudging out to drag the rusty hand-mower back and forth across the spotty lawn, as there was no question of my father assuming that task.

But in June, on her birthday, the rosebush on the trellis would spring into a mass of messy, luxuriant blooms. Its disordered, sensuous state had nothing to do with my mother, but every year I hoped the roses would mean something to her. Perhaps they alone would bring her pleasure. I wished she would bury her nose in the hot pink ruffles of the roses, pick them and fill vases with bouquets. But she was not a celebratory kind of person.

On her daughters' birthdays she gave us what we asked for, no more, no less. There was always the requisite gathering with friends from school who came for tea and party favors like sugared candies in a crepe paper basket and a cake covered with fat sickeningly-sweet roses.

For her own birthday we fussed over what to give her, eager to produce some magical surprise that would somehow stir her out of her measured pose of dignified motherhood. I made her sachets, but then that meant I had to ask her for the recipe. Orrisroot and rose talc made a lot of slippery powder when they were measured out at Mr. Motorano's drugstore. Mummy had to help me thread the needle, but in the end she said the lumpy package was all she wanted, as she laid it away unnoticed in her bureau drawer.

My father brought her presents but they never had much to do with my mother. They seemed more to his taste. Paté in tins, splits of champagne, once a dainty saucer of a hat made of fine Panama straw. But it was too small. We were all allowed to try it on in the vain hope it would fit someone, as my father kept muttering under his breath how expensive it had been.

When my mother turned forty, her own mother clearly glimpsed how she might be feeling. Gran gave her a ring of her own with three stones, two sapphires and a diamond in the middle. The stones were so large they were set on the vertical. My grandmother said, "It's because you're my third child," but I believed it was because she knew how old and gray my mother felt.

But on her fortieth birthday, I was not there for that familiar tea party. As an emerging teenager, I was beginning to let my own desires, however secret, surface. I trespassed against unspoken sibling rules (we must be there to fete Mummy) and I didn't show up. Instead, I went to the movies with Jonathan Silverman, necking in the balcony of the UT theater in Harvard Square. It was a double feature of *On the Waterfront* and *From Here to Eternity*, a sop to the Harvard boys who were celebrating the end of finals.

I went in full knowledge that I was breaking two cardinal rules. First, I had broken the vow of sisterly solidarity, and, second, I had betrayed my mother. I was doing what I wanted to do, something she never did herself. I had put someone else, primarily myself, ahead of my mother and her sacred day. When I came home, feeling as moist and sexy as Deborah Kerr in her clinging bathing suit, I snuck into my mother's bedroom. "I'm sorry I missed your party," I gulped, feeling guilty and exhausted from the effort of defiance.

"Darling," she said, as she put her arm around me, "I want you to have fun."

Take Me Out to the Ball Game

My father was the talker in my family—when he wanted to be. There were plenty of silent family dinners. If he was bored, not with us exactly, only the irksome role of being a traditional pater familias, he would read a book at supper. When each of us reached the sixth grade at twelve, we were invited to eat in the dining room with my parents. We sat formally arranged around the dark rectangular table. There was too much room between each of us. Also in the dining room along with the somber furniture was the only telephone on the first floor. There it sat, a squat sentinel and witness to a family that didn't communicate. If the telephone rang during dinner, we girls were not allowed to say anything more than "I can't talk; when can I call you back?" The telephone's ring was a merry reminder that there was life outside the tension of the dining room.

When my father was in a good mood, perhaps soothed by a swat of gin, he was beguilingly open, full of stories, gossip, funny memories of childhood. "At St. Bernard's, in the fourth grade

I was Ceres, mother of the harvest," he reported once, and we all laughed, so curious it was, even to him, that he—my erratic, spoiled father—should be cast as a serene Earth Mother. Once, he flew the coop, on a lazy summer trip to cruise with a college friend in the Aegean. He sent a postcard from Athens inscribed "The Acropolis is fine and I am beautiful." Nothing is funny in the retelling. It is more the knowledge that with him I knew I would laugh, that it was okay, if not necessary, to laugh.

A book called *Fractured French* encapsulated my father's sense of the ridiculous. There, French idiomatic expressions were satirically translated. "Pied-à-terre" showed a man in a tuxedo turning his back on his dinner guests to relieve himself in the bushes. "Carte Blanche" showed a tipsy floozy being helped from a party. Beneath it was the caption, "For God's sake, why doesn't someone take Blanche home?" The illustrations were by a *New Yorker* favorite, Peter Arno (I felt an affinity right from the start for the *New Yorker*, as it was something both my parents enjoyed). Arno's gleeful, slashing line of drawings skewered the urbane world my father knew well.

A couple in evening clothes peering into the nursery before going out to a dinner party, and murmuring to each other, "Hmm, I thought we had five," was the *New Yorker* cartoon that made my father laugh. He loved making fun of people who had everything, people who took themselves too seriously.

My father could not, would not, enter into family life except as a wayward, dashing suitor. He liked to go out, to be seen, to feel exhilarated in a crowd of friends and admirers. In contrast to my mother, my father thrived on celebration. He felt it was his right to be happy, to be noticed and to be appreciated.

Occasionally, very occasionally, he would rescue my mother from cooking yet another leg of lamb for yet another Sunday lunch. (Why did she stick so to those old-fashioned routines? She was the cook and the decision maker. Why didn't she rebel? Did she want us to appear a conventional family as much as I did?)

My father didn't care about proper family lunches at home, but he did like a treat at the Ritz hotel in Boston. We would file into the big upstairs dining room where the blue water glasses glowed on the white linen tabletops and the long windows gave out onto the leafy Public Garden. Once the maitre d'hotel stopped us. My father didn't have on a tie, just his weekend corduroys and a rough tweed jacket. "Lend me your tie," rallied my father, and the waiter did. Later he told my father he was funnier than Danny Kaye.

Daddy (as I describe these scenes, occasionally my father slips into more traditional roles and I slip into calling him, as I once did, "Daddy") would sometimes court me as the good middle daughter to accompany him on a spree to a restaurant, or an art gallery, or a cocktail party at a friend's house. In truth I preferred to stay at home, but I wanted to please and I wanted to be with him. He had a Willys Jeepster—black, loud and snappy which he drove fast, recklessly, badly. "No one has passed me yet," he flashed out at me proudly while I huddled in my seat, praying we would make it back to dull, reassuring safety. The schoolboy playing hooky, he sang off-key, "Take me out to the ball game, take me out to the park ... I don't care if we never get back ..."

FPK at a Harvard football game, c. 1956

For my father, the reason for leaving the house was to pursue pleasure. He was an avid Harvard undergraduate sports fan, religiously attending football matches on hazy autumn afternoons, and in the spring, baseball games and track meets. At these less-popular events we would often be among the few spectators in the stadium. Mr. Gummere, a Harvard colleague of my father's, sometimes joined us in the empty stands. He could recite from Aeschylus and one day gave me one of his translations, inscribed on the flyleaf to "Miss Maisie Kinnicutt, in memory of happy afternoons." I savored being alone with these two nostalgic, middle-aged men, surrounded as we were by dazzling athletes in the bright, fleeting light of spring. I studied the program, carefully scrutinizing the resolute, square-jawed faces of the young sportsmen, plotting a fantasy of romance with each one.

I learned more about running the hurdles, and even about classical Greek poetry, from being with Mr. Gummere than from being with my father. My father didn't like to give explanations. Far too restless, only the enjoyment of the moment counted.

As he grew older and began to inwardly challenge the prescribed patterns of his youth, he grew curious and confident about his eye for modern art. In the pocket diary from his early married life, there is no mention of visiting a gallery or a museum. It is all about boxing matches and late-night drinking in smoky bars, going to the country for the weekend and wishing he didn't have to be a Wall Street lawyer. But Cambridge and its rock-ribbed faith in the "life of the mind" gave him the courage to pursue the sudden rapport he felt when he saw a picture by Picasso or Braque or Matisse. The books piled up— Herbert Read, James Thrall Soby, catalogues from the Museum of Modern Art, particularly heavy, illustrated books on Picasso, his hero. He commissioned a young architectural student from the Harvard Graduate School of Design to copy Picasso's *Three Musicians* onto the cement outer wall of the garage that formed one side of our Larch Road backyard. His correspondence to friends was written on postcards of Miró or Klee or Toulouse-Lautrec.

He began to buy small contemporary pictures for himself. A drawing by Mark Tobey, watercolors of Lionel Feininger and Elie Nadelman, a tiny, haunting Joseph Cornell box. Nothing big or dramatic, his choices dictated as much by price as by taste, he never paid more than a few hundred dollars for a picture. Once he found a Pollock gouache for $250 and was thrilled with himself ten years later when he sold it for $10,000.

New paintings with odd subjects, unclear forms and disturbing color combinations sprouted about our house like unexpected exotica in a traditional English perennial border.

They perturbed me. There was a copy of Picasso's *Blue Boy* over my bed, a rosy-cheeked nude lady above the sideboard in the dining room. My mother's nineteenth-century hunting prints went to the attic and Henry Moore's mournful underground figures stood guard in the hall. I felt they were telling us something. Beware: what you see is not what you think you know.

When my father bought a Picasso etching of an artist in his studio drawing a voluptuous model with a bull leering in the background, he scrawled in his notes, "I hope to God it's not a fake." For my part, I hoped this madness would soon end.

Daddy's primary beat was New York City, especially the Downtown Gallery or Betty Parsons' gallery on East 57th Street. Perhaps it was another excuse to flee home and responsibility, but it was also his answer to his own father, a stern and didactic collector of Early American furniture, English Lowestoft china and embroidered wall samplers and fire screens. It was the same breaking with tradition that inspired my father's sister, whom he nicknamed "Sister" to paint her heavy mahogany furniture white and her floors red. (She eventually became known as Sister Parish, the much sought after decorator whom Jackie Kennedy claimed to help decorate the White House. It prompted the headline that made my father laugh, "Nun to decorate the White House.") These Kinnicutts were possessed by a similar desire to seek out the different, the unrecognized. All three—my father, his father and his sister—shared an instinctive eagerness to embellish, to create, to make their mark in the more conventional world in which they had chosen to live. They were blessed with that same elusive thing called "an eye," just as they were all cursed with the same irascibly short temper.

Sometimes I kept my father company on his prowls through the few Boston contemporary art galleries that existed. I found those Saturday afternoons long, the basement rooms chilly and the paintings incomprehensible, but I wanted to be loyal to him even if I dreaded being with him. Once he knew he had someone at his side, someone mute, adoring, untroubling, he would wander off, chatting up gallery owners who would be huddled in their overcoats in the back room, and swapping gossip with any friend he happened to encounter. He never explained his passion, but then I never asked. I was afraid of acting too interested, for then I would be trapped.

The first "modern" picture my father ever bought was a snake around the sun by Morris Graves. He carried it into the house himself and hung it triumphantly over my mother's favorite sofa in the back sitting room. "There, this is modern art, what do you think, May-Day?" he asked me defiantly.

My mother on her favorite sofa;
Snake around the Sun *by Morris Graves hangs above, 1956*

Recoiling from the flat brooding calm of mustard yellows and blurry grey, I was instantly uneasy. This was change. This was temptation. This was another place from which my mother would be excluded.

The back sitting room with its bay window and fireplace was the central axis of our Larch Road life. This sitting room was considered my mother's space. Here she had placed her grandmother's furniture, the cane-back sofa from Wheatly that she insisted had been made by Mr. Davenport himself for her

Frankie Kinnicutt, c. 1945

grandparents, the delicate painted chair, the three-tiered what-not table that held her dictionary and a much-mended china bowl filled with browning potpourri.

But when my father placed the picture over her favorite sofa, I realized I had read the signals wrong. My mother wanted my father there. She was proud of his eye, of his daring and imagination in seeing that Graves and Cornell and Henry Moore were guides for us to live by. He was as exotic and compelling as the pictures on the wall. These paintings were different. There was some withheld meaning to them. Did I object to the paintings because they were strange and different, or because they took him away?

As the room began to be transformed by these elusive hieroglyphs of paintings, there was always one picture that stayed in the same spot. It was a photograph of my father, in a white torn t-shirt, sitting in a wooden outdoor chair with the afternoon light of summer like a halo around him. It remained permanently on a table by the chair my father preferred when he was present, however momentarily, in this room. Was it my mother's small private talisman to encourage her that he would always return? Now it sits on my desk, but it took me a long time to allow his flashy allure into my private space; I had deemed it too personal, too threatening.

—⚏—

Only once, at around the age of ten, did I consciously invade my parents' arena, that tense region where they dwelt and around which I picked my careful way. It was Memorial Day weekend. I hated Memorial Day; it signaled the end of that safe haven, school. It was not that I was so clever at school or that I had so many friends. It was only that everything there was sane and predictable. There were the prescribed hoops to jump through and I did so—neatly, quietly, competently. I eschewed making trouble, no matter how much I wanted to be noticed. But on that particular Memorial Day I suddenly decided to make a flamboyant bid for attention.

Mummy, who was never one for surprises, told me on Friday

night that she and Daddy would be taking off the next day to spend the night with cousins on the North Shore, an hour or so up the coast from Boston. The thought of a long, listless weekend with my sisters, scrapping over comic books and over whose turn it was to fetch Good Humor bars from the ice-cream wagon, staggered me. I refused to be left to the mournful sound of the bass drum floating up from Fresh Pond Parkway as the straggling parade of red-faced veterans wove its way from Mt. Auburn cemetery. What enormous dose of arrogance bolstered me as I did the unthinkable and opened the door to my parents' bedroom early that Saturday morning?

"You can't go," I announced firmly into the darkness, to the two vague mounds who were my parents, lying with their backs turned toward each other.

"What do you mean?" stammered my mother, alert, awake and still in bed. "We've had this planned for weeks. We're going to Dede and Henry's housewarming. We'll be back tomorrow afternoon. What is this fuss you're making?"

"You can't go," I repeated, appalled at my own daring.

What did I want them to do, except of course to perform that one startling act of noticing me? In the end it was a compromise. They went to Dede and Henry's party, but they took me with them.

I didn't realize then what a compromise it was. I was staggered by my success. Was this all it took to be paid attention to? To invade dangerous territory, expect the explosion but then instead of a wound or even a reversal, to be handed a reward instead?

Begrudgingly, in deference to my propensity for car sickness,

I was wedged in the front seat of the car between my parents, my mother at the wheel because Daddy's driving made everyone, including himself, nervous. Now I was the hump of discord between my parents, but we were off on a trip to the thinner, lighter air of the North Shore, to Beverly, the three of us alone for the first time I could remember. I had escaped Memorial Day.

Henry was a younger cousin of Daddy's, significant only in his callow blondness and his ability to make money. He had a big white house on the water and a pretty wife called Dede. She in turn had a wide gap-toothed smile and a sapphire ring the color of her blue eyes. "Henry said it had to match," she giggled. I inspected Dede and her ring coolly, privately loyal to my mother and her discreet band of small diamonds. "Never make a show" was her credo, but now I was treading in different waters.

I wandered about in limbo at the party, too young for the grown-ups beginning to gather on the big veranda with Japanese lanterns and furniture of rococo wrought iron, but too old for my small cousins, already in their pajamas. Deep down I knew how out of place I was, but I was determined to pull off this invasion of my parents' territory. Again I felt that compulsion to protect my mother. Parties were a kind of agony for her. She didn't speak the language of spontaneity and flirtation. She hung back with me, a slight shadow at her side.

But I was drawn to my father, so in his element, so at home with banter and laughter and drinking. He was surrounded by people, mostly women, all pretty and young. Of course my mother with her dark eyes and slender figure was pretty too, but she didn't act as though she felt pretty.

He called over to me, "Hey, Maizel-Daizel" (which was what he called me when he was in a good mood), "Essie here thinks you look like me."

I turned to take in Essie, coquettish in white silk pleated culottes and wedged high heels. I would have preferred to look like her more than anyone, particularly when Daddy stepped back to watch her trip away. But I secretly glowed to think that anyone would consider my father and me as the same beast—we who were so clearly opposite, he with his bravado, me always in the background with my head down. Now someone had seen it. We were alike, we were allies.

Then something even more surprising happened. Swirling his drink, gripping the highball glass, Daddy murmured to his glass and to me, "No one here can hold a candle to your mother. She's the only person in the room with class."

Dumbfounded and radiant that my father had acknowledged not only me but my mother as well, I wanted to quit this scene of triumph, to leave it perfect, intact. I drifted away from the party, hugging this discovery to myself.

My mother found me on the dock.

"I'm sorry I made such a fuss," I said, repentant in happiness.

"That's alright, but I wouldn't try such a stunt if you ever want to get something out of your husband," she teased.

"Like what, what would I want?" I asked, ever curious as to what mysterious ingredient could help along a marriage.

"Oh, I don't know," she mused, my mother who never asked anybody for anything, let alone my father. "Maybe a mink coat," she laughed at herself, smiling into the blue night.

The next day was a fall from Eden. I lay too long on that same dock, drunk on the sun, on my newfound power, on the breezy luxury of Henry's and Dede's big house. When it was time to leave, I was hot and flushed from my own abandon.

"You've had too much sun," clucked my mother crossly.

"Too much of a good thing," leered Henry.

"Just like all of us," snarled my father, his mood a violent switch from the night before.

As we were driving home I began to feel carsick. Holiday traffic surrounded us, stymieing even my mother, always the skillful driver. But she was most intent on avoiding my father's mounting temper. Once home, I collapsed on the stairwell.

"For God's sake, won't someone do something with this child?" demanded my father, as he pushed past me on his way upstairs to lie down himself.

Things were back to normal.

Dark Harbor Fancy Dress

There is one time I remember my father being patient.

My mother was the one to teach me how to cope with life's practical exigencies: to tie my shoes, to tell the time, to ride a bicycle. My father couldn't be bothered with imparting such small, significant details but there was one surprise: he did teach me to row a boat. He was so impatient it impressed me that he took the time. It was a proper lesson that day, that summer of being eleven. First he showed me how to sit in the middle of the seat to avoid tipping, how to unhinge the oarlocks from their stations, to slide the oars up from under the seat and then to slowly, evenly, and assuredly (all those virtues my father had trouble dealing with) lift them up. "Now out, down, deep into the still water, wait (something he could never do), let the boat glide. Pull, but not too hard on one side, don't jerk, keep it on an even keel."

There was something soothing about the water. Having spent summers in Maine, he wanted to return often to his childhood happiness. The biggest surprise in learning to row a boat is that if you are the rower, you sit with your back in the direction you are going. To reach your destination you turn your back to it. You trust it will still be there. You trust yourself as you dip your oars into the smooth water. Of course, you allow yourself swift glances over your shoulder, but my father said, "You always sit with your back to where you are headed."

But it was more the lure of being there alone, guided and protected by my father, gazing spellbound at his handsomeness, his flash of a grin, his green eyes, his brown legs stretched out on either side of me in the shell of the boat. I later tell this story to my aunt, his sister.

"Oh, but he was hopeless in a boat, so reckless, so foolhardy."

Still I hug the memory to myself because it was the one time he behaved like everyone else's father, the masterful parent, rowing his young daughter home.

So this memory is his gift: his presence in a place that mattered very much in my childhood and is still a thread of life that I treasure. In the summers my father brought us to Dark Harbor, a real place, an actual safe harbor, in Penobscot Bay on an island called Islesboro, three miles off the coast of Maine.

Islesboro, a long curling leaf of an island, a sliver of rock and pine, hovers close to the mainland. But not too close. Its residents have always prided themselves on its being different from other islands of Penobscot Bay. Myriad as stars, these islands speckle the bay. Some of these islands are substantial, sheltering prosperous summer resorts or hardy fishing communities throughout every season. Others are craggy heaps of barnacled rock. Stunningly beautiful, each has a familiar, almost monotonous tapestry of evergreen forest and stony beach. But even though the scenery might be the same, Islesboro residents were different. There was always something ornery about people on Islesboro.

"These are our ways," people in the village would say when they voted to keep the school open even for eighty students, or to limit the use of the airstrip. "Our children are better-looking," I remember a friend of my mother's reporting when she came back from a visit to the mainland, even though summer offspring were often nearly identical, with blond towheads and smooth tanned skin. Summer people and island people, together we were all a little spoiled. We believed some small nugget of us was different because of island life, island difficulties, island beauty.

Even the very name "Islesboro" was cover. The real place my family and I and my friends wanted to reach was not just Islesboro, but Dark Harbor—a tiny pinprick of a cove on the southern end of the spindly island. There are lots of other places to summer on the island, like Pripet and Ryder's Cove and Sabbath Day Harbor, but I am still unsure of the whereabouts of those other places. My whole intent every summer, was to return to Dark Harbor and to find it the same. My sisters and I knew the Rachel Field poem, "If Once You Have Slept on an Island," with its defining last line, "But once you have slept on an island, You'll never be quite the same." In our family of three sisters and parents who lived together but were estranged, Islesboro was the one constant.

Of course the island was always the same. It was we who were changing. I returned each year in June, after the discipline of school in a New England winter of icicles and dirty March snow. When I came back to the island on those first nights, my sisters and I ran through the house to inspect each room, pulling last year's leftover dresses over our scabby knees, laughing at life preservers that hit hard under the arms. It seemed that nothing in my old bedroom or on the island had changed. The same grey-blue periwinkle shells collected from last summer on the bureau, the same splintered floats in the harbor where we had tried to learn to swim the year before, the bell buoy tolling at night in the fog, the blue Camden Hills, the tide at the Narrows creeping in and out.

Islesboro's very inconvenience gave it allure and cachet. To get there is still an adventure. A standard greeting on arrival is often, "When did you get here?" and "How long will you stay?" No one means to be unwelcoming, only to imply they recognize the trouble one has gone to to make the journey to Islesboro.

When Dark Harbor was discovered as a summer community in the late nineteenth century, there was a steamer that trundled up the coast from Boston. Horse and carriage met passengers at Lime Kiln Wharf on the north side of the island. Until the thirties, no cars were allowed on the island. My mother remembered arriving for a visit with her mother, who thought it important that her daughters "meet boys"—not to marry, they were only fourteen or so at the time—but in order to have fun and travel beyond the secluded countryside of rural Long Island. My mother was proud because my grandmother could drive the rented horse and buggy herself. She had grown up around horses and didn't need one of Mr. Hale's stable boys to help her.

This family of three Jay women spent two weeks in Dark Harbor at the Islesboro Inn, a large, rambling hotel atop a high, wooded bluff. The Inn, silvery and majestic with its weathered shingles and black-green rocking chairs spread along the wide expanse of columned porch, faced the East Bay. Which way you face has always been important for island life. At the Inn with its long stretch of porch, you got the morning sun (but not the newspapers at breakfast because they didn't, and still don't, arrive until the afternoon). Still, you could always go to a friend's house on the "Gold Coast," which faced west, for tea after the end of the sailboat races to sit silently and watch the sun set over the big arc of the Camden hills.

My mother didn't meet my father that summer of 1928. He was older and considered "wild," but a decade later they were married, becoming frequent visitors to my father's parents on Kinnicutt Point. The house on the point, perched on its own little promontory of rock and cedar and spruce, facing due west toward the Camden Hills, was incongruously modeled after an Austrian hunting lodge with thick white stucco walls and red shutters carved with hearts. My father had grown up in this house. It had been built as a present for his grandmother by her rich brother, who lived in a larger, grander house on another neighboring curve of the point. As a child I somehow had the misapprehension that my father's family had suffered a reversal of fortune, and this little cottage was where they ignominiously ended up. This vague sense of financial malaise was nonsense, part of confused Dark Harbor family folklore.

But I think my father encouraged that fantasy. He saw himself as odd man out, tilting against windmills. He loved Dark Harbor, he loved the good life, the lavish old ways of houses with servants and rooms full of flowers and plenty of invitations for the evening's entertainment. But he indulged that Kinnicutt desire to be outside the box, to be just a little bit different from his neighbors. A symbol of this sense of specialness—however misplaced—was Thrumcap, a minute fleck of an island, rooted in the narrow channel that runs past his family house.

Thrumcap is a natural fortress of rock and trees. At low tide a dinghy can be dragged up the muddy spit of beach and safely left while you climb up the embankment, clutching at spruce branches as your sneakered feet slide over crumbling slate. Once secure on a slight crest of earth, you are in a private kingdom of moss and fern and bayberry. No one can see you from the water or from the great neighboring houses.

As a boy, my father must have studied this dot of an island from his bedroom window. It was his place to go to on his own. He could row there with his friends or by himself. Thrumcap was tiny, a mere ten yards or so long and not that wide, but it was his, his private domain, his fiefdom. Later, as young men, he and his brother held drinks parties at noon, where the point of the morning was to see who could stride out onto the lawn, put down his glass of iced tea with rum, and smack a golf ball across the narrow inlet. There were bets on who could land his ball on the shore or, best yet, at the unseen center of Thrumcap.

Now, almost a hundred years after the house was built and my father grew up in its red-shuttered privacy, there is—at his request—a stone of granite on Thrumcap set back amidst the pines and scrub. It reads, "In memory of Frankie Kinnicutt. He loved this island." People tell me they sail by "that island where your father is buried." Somehow I am irritated by this misperception.

He did not claim the island as his private burial ground. In fact it never belonged to his family anyway and now has been deeded to the Islesboro Island Trust, "forever wild," an apt description of my father himself. Daddy only wanted Thrumcap recognized as the scene of fleeting happiness.

By 1937, when my parents were married, the old steamer service was gone. The war came, and many of the big houses on the Gold Coast remained closed summer after summer. When I came to Dark Harbor for the first time at the age of five, we stayed in the village in an islander's house with hand-knitted afghans and white painted iron bedsteads. Sybil and I, outfitted in matching pastel sundresses, were sent up the hill to pay a call on my grandmother, my father's mother, who was by then a frail-seeming widow of sixty. She spent the summer at the "Little Inn," another spacious summer house with an endless porch. It served as a substitute for the big old inn, now shut for the duration of the war.

Grandma Kinnicutt was sitting on the porch, dressed on this summer day in a straight linen skirt with a cashmere sweater trimmed in grosgrain ribbon, all three pieces of the same pale beige color. I leaned forward to kiss her cheek. Her powder and faint perfume mingled with the scent of the sweet peas from the hotel garden. I wanted to feel a special bond with her. I had been christened May; I was her namesake.

Grandma Kinnicutt started out on the right foot.

"Darling," she mumured. Her hand of brown spots and blue veins lingered over mine. I liked being called "darling." It was the age of endearments. Tizzy's nurse implored us to be "sweethearts." My aunt called us "pet." Our favorite joke when asked to do an errand was "Be an angel … and go upstairs."

"I have a little something for you," she said in her low drawl of a voice. Sybil, and the sisterly loyalty I felt toward her, seemed to dissolve in the warm afternoon air. Perhaps Sybil already had received something precious; I don't remember, but I badly wanted my "something."

Barely looking at me, Grandma handed me, with her habitual lazy flop of a gesture, a slender white box. Inside was a silver teaspoon with "our" initials, an *M* and a *K* spiraling up its handle. The letters were entwined with the outlines of leaves and flowering vines. My magpie heart leapt up. I loved being singled out from my sisters, but later, I was disgusted with Grandma. Back home, on closer inspection, I discovered in the monogram an unwanted *A*. Didn't she know my name was different, ever so slightly, from hers? She was May Appleton, I was called Maisie. I had inherited the ornery island spirit.

Shortly afterwards, in the late 1940s, this grandmother died and my father, feeling flush, bought a house in the village for $2,000. We were to come regularly every summer to Islesboro for the next ten years.

That first year at the end of June, my mother piled us sisters, along with Beau, our aging whippet, and the flat silver (de rigueur for Dark Harbor dinner parties) into her grey Studebaker and made the six-hour trip up from Cambridge. The battered inheritance of a Vuitton trunk, which had sat in the front hall for a month, was gradually stocked up with heavy sweaters, books for summer reading and rubber bathing shoes for swimming off the rocks. It had been sent up on the train to Rockland, Maine. Mr. Leach, the island delivery man, would bring it over to Dark Harbor from Rockland on his truck, which he called "Ma Jackie."

By 1951, our first full summer on Islesboro, the way to reach the island was aboard a sturdy new ferry, the *Governor Brann*, which chugged back and forth across the West Bay six times daily: it had become a twenty-minute journey from Lincolnville Beach. Lincolnville was a strip of sand bordered by touristy lobster restaurants and boardinghouses, just off a crowded two-lane highway and about twenty miles north of Rockland. Anticipation began to churn when we hit Rockland, a declining industrial town of stone quarries and fishing boats, but there were still those twenty miles to go. The games of Ghost or Man, woman, boy or girl? drifted off. The last half-hour up the coast on U.S. Route 1, a dusty, trafficky bit from Rockland, was the slowest. We drove through prosperous, pristine Camden, the car inching past heavy trucks and meandering visitors who paused at every glimpse of water. Then suddenly my mother swooped off the main road with a little jagged turn down to the ferry landing with its granite piers and patch of beach and swept the car into the reservation line. She smoothed her skirt and took a swig from the gingerale bottle she kept on hand for anyone apt to feel carsick. "Plenty of time for the three o'clock," she murmured proudly to herself. We tumbled out of the car. Almost stunned

Our house in Dark Harbor, Maine, c. 1950

with the soft air that was heavy with the wet seaweed and wild rose that lined the roads in summer, we began to look for anyone we knew waiting in line for the next ferry. The summer, that first summer when we came as true residents, not guests of my grandmother or at the Inn, had begun.

The house we lived in then was by the shaded pool on the main village road. This pool was the original "Dark Harbor." The story we children were told was that the original eighteenth-century settlers had sailed into a particularly gloomy cove on Islesboro, and exclaimed, "Oh, what a dark harbor!" I used to imagine them, looking like the Pilgrims we pretended to be in school plays, dressed in black and white, their prim mouths forming a polite unison of "oh."

Rosa rugosa grew in tangled, thorny barriers in front of our low, white house. It had once been a farm cottage but had been added to so many times by various prosperous owners that it stretched across the rise of the apple orchard on which it perched. By the time my parents bought it, it was a bit shabby, sagging under the weight of so many additions. Grass grew up through the brick walks. Queen Anne's lace had taken over the tennis court. My mother still dragged hampers of beach towels and pillow cases to the adjacent laundry house with its deep stone sinks, but the maids' rooms became a private clubhouse for us children, with plenty of space to give plays in which we staggered about in swaths of forgotten muslin curtains.

Going to Maine for the summer, three golden months of it, was supposed to teach us, my sisters and me, three city girls, about nature and outdoor life. We were meant to grow accustomed to being on the water, specifically sailing, or in it, swimming. We were made to take lessons in swimming (quickly abandoned because the water was so cold), then in tennis. Mr. Klingeman, the patient tennis pro, drew little boxes in the brick-red sand of the courts to show us where we should stand to serve a ball. "Spread your wings and scratch your back," he urged us. At the end of the lesson our racquets were taped to remind us where to place our thumbs for the backhand swing.

Finally, and most incomprehensibly, there were lessons in sailing where we never set foot on a boat but squatted on the dock with the young college-age instructor as he struggled to teach us to tie a bowline knot using the trick of "chasing the fox through the rabbit hole".

I wish I could say that I learned about boats and the backhand and diving, but I didn't. I eschewed the rough-and-tumble of organized activity. Ignoring friendly harbor life, with outboard motors buzzing back and forth to neighborly docks, I bobbled happily about, like one of the sturdy dinghies tied to the club float, nudging my way ever so gently, ever so persistently into other people's lives.

In Dark Harbor, family life with its intricacies and passions beat out even our favorite make-believe stories such as the soap operas, like *Our Gal Sunday* and *One Man's Family* that Sybil and I listened to back in Cambridge. Certainly outdoor life played second-string to the mysteries and secrets abounding in Dark Harbor during those summers. What we did during those summers in Dark Harbor was minimal. What we noticed was a lot.

In our house, there was a set of stairs that led directly off the front sitting room. I could perch there in the evenings unseen and listen to the hazy buzz of conversation between my parents and their friends. One night I heard them fussing over someone who was having trouble making sense. I turned it over in my head on who this might be, perhaps lithe Ellen Fife, who had recently arrived on the island. Certainly not my father's cousin, crisp, clearheaded Aunt Ibbie. There were murmurings and importunings, and suddenly dead silence. Then I heard my mother laugh in relief. "Well, Ibbie, this is ridiculous but now that we've got Ellen settled, would you like a drink?" The next morning I asked my mother point-blank if Mrs. Fife had been drunk.

Angel Hollins with her mother, "Aunt Ibbie," c. 1950

"I think she was exhausted. She passed out, a dead weight, and I needed Aunt Ibbie to help me put her to bed."

Aunt Ibbie was my father's oldest friend on the island. They were first cousins and had grown up together and still frolicked in happy consort as though they were still children. Aunt Ibbie, in contrast to my mother, was blonde and determined, with a habit of turning the corners of her mouth down and jutting her chin up in a haughty thrust when she wanted to make her point.

One night at someone's dinner party, there was a tapping on the window. "Kids," scoffed the host, but it was Daddy and Ibbie creeping through the dark, playing "spy," to check out who was where. Later they drank champagne and bounced on a neighbor's trampoline. Thus it was unusual for my mother to be so chummy with Aunt Ibbie, perennial rival that she was.

No one in Dark Harbor appeared to live with their immediate family. Children came to stay with grandparents, stepmothers, aunts and uncles. Aunt Ibbie's daughter, Angel, was my best friend. Her parents had divorced and Aunt Ibbie had remarried. Angel and her sisters docilely shuttled back and forth between her two parents, an enviable position, I thought. Now at Aunt Ibbie's, there was a new baby. Angel and I were sent on walks with Mademoiselle, the governess for Angel and her older sisters.

Mademoiselle added greatly to my story repertoire. "I have a *petite histoire* for you girls," she would announce after we settled ourselves on the rocky beach. I was never quite sure if these stories had happened to Mademoiselle herself or to someone in her acquaintance. My heart turned over at the pain of the young bride who sold her hair to buy a watch chain for her husband, when, lo and behold, he had just pawned his watch to buy her hair combs. And what about the poor woman who lost her friend's pearl necklace and worked all her life to pay her back, only to discover it had been paste?

"What's 'paste'?" demanded practical Angel. "*Pas pour ta maman,*" sniffed Mademoiselle, struggling to her feet. "Now we go home," she commanded, suddenly all business. As we walked home through the dusty fields, she produced battered tin cans with holes bored in their sides and string run through the holes. This way we could wear the cans around our necks, and our hands would be free to pick and eat berries at the same time.

Clearly Mademoiselle wanted to show Aunt Ibbie she had done more for us than give a lurid précis of de Maupassant. We ambled slowly along, the ripe blackberries hitting the empty cans with a satisfying splat.

My mother professed to loathe gossip, but on walks with her friend Mrs. Biddle, who placed a pebble on her head to improve her posture, my mother and I both listened carefully to her idle chitchat. The woods, the smell of cedar and bayberry, the crunch of pinecone, and mussel shell fallen from a seagull's mouth were the silent background for the tales she told as we traipsed along behind her single file.

"Once, on one of my treks, I came out upon Crow Cove and what did I see but the bootlegger's skiff crammed with whiskey bottles. I went straight to Eben Randlett and demanded to know just what was going on. He looked sheepish, but muttered something about, 'Oh Mrs. B., you wouldn't be wanting our men to be drinking vanilla, would you?'."

Drinking played a large part in summer lives. Everyone seemed to be drinking all the time. The cocktail hour with everyone gathering on the porch or around the fire with the curtains drawn against the fog, marked the end of a boisterous, hearty day, and the entrance of the blue-velvet night. There was sherry after church, and rum in the iced tea at Mrs. Leonard's after the Twenties' race, and on afternoon picnics our mothers carried a thermos of watery martinis.

The dusky barroom at the Inn, with its curved-back wicker chairs set up around card tables, was a center of boozy connection and camaraderie. The Inn had declined since my parents' youth. But it was still a symbol of "the way things used to be": the rockers on the porch and the separate dining rooms, one for the grown-ups and one for the children with their nurses, nannies and tutors. The ordered tenor of life in Dark Harbor began with its carefully appointed hours: mornings for lessons, golf games and ladies' tennis matches; Wednesday and Saturday afternoons for sailing races; Saturday evening for big "pay-back" dinner parties and eleven o'clock church on Sunday with Mr. Kellogg, slightly hungover from a late Saturday night party, coming over from nearby Minot Island in his cassock and rubber-soled boat shoes.

The most exciting ritual of the summer, from my standpoint was the Fancy Dress Ball, where grown-ups and children alike appeared in costume, and the grand finale of the night was a tipsy parade of all the prizewinners. The whole point of the Fancy Dress was to be inventive, spontaneous, and certainly never to appear as though you had planned your getup in advance. The first one I remember took place at the Inn shortly before it was torn down. A penny postcard arrived in our mailbox a few days before announcing the theme: "Come as you were fifteen years ago or will be in fifteen years." I was ten and ran home to drag out limp muslin curtains from the musty linen closet to rig myself up as a bride, adding fifteen years to my ten and hoping privately I would be married well before twenty-five. My mother and her sister Theo, on the island for a visit, suddenly threw themselves into the spirit of make-believe that afternoon. Windblown and sunburnt from sailing, they poured themselves stiff bourbons and retired to my parents' bedroom, only to

Aunt Theo and my mother, c. 1952

re-appear, statuesque and giggling, in Sybil's and my matching sundresses, their full bosoms straining across the smocked tops. "I hope people don't think *we* think we looked like this fifteen years ago," murmured Theo.

Hardly ever did my mother behave so unexpectedly. She was too prudent and guarded, and had never felt at home in Dark

Harbor. It was my father's bailiwick, the playground where he shone, where he was petted and admired just as he had been while a little boy. My mother didn't seem to have any close friends amidst the Dark Harbor cliques; the women her age had known each other, and my father, since childhood. She submitted to the daily tennis game, but didn't chat or gossip afterwards with these women. "Sybil is so steady," was the begrudging compliment they bestowed on my mother.

My father came home late from parties, and I could hear them arguing behind the closed bedroom door. By the 1950s, any feeling of warmth had petered out between my parents, and my mother resented the summer community she had inherited along with her unhappy marriage.

"What I hate about Dark Harbor is always having to change my clothes," I heard her snarl under her breath as she jerked open a bureau drawer. The white tennis dress, the gloves and straw hat for church, the long dress for the evening, these were all part of the ritual, the pattern, the "way things used to be." (Ironically, my father usually outfitted himself in unorthodox attire: a striped French sailor's shirt, khaki shorts held up by a narrow necktie, espadrilles for day, and at night, velvet slippers proudly monogrammed "FPK.")

As a child, I sensed that my parents were trying to do their duty, trying to hold on to what didn't exist, just as the summer people of Dark Harbor were trying to hold on to what also had vanished. The careless, palmy days of the twenties and the Gold Coast were gone. My father, who wasn't a snob, proudly noted, "Everyone in Dark Harbor is a lady and a gentleman." But they were ghostly figures. The Dark Harbor of the early fifties was a faded, crumbling version of its former self. Houses were closed, deserted; people had moved away. Though still remarkably well-heeled, those who returned each summer talked poor. They complained about the high prices at the village market (though you could still call up and have a lemon or a lobster or a box of Wheat Thins delivered to your kitchen pantry), they let the boat captain go, they sighed over the island girls who couldn't (or wouldn't) wait on table, and they grimly pulled dust covers over chaise longues in the "big room."

Despite the powerful charm of those blazing blue afternoons, watching the race on someone's big motorboat, or being lulled by the sense of security that came with eyeing large families squeeze into their church pews each Sunday, something sad lingered, however faint. Despite the patina of abundance and continuity, there was the presence of loss. For all the privilege, all the enforced jollity of having a "good time," people on Islesboro seemed to have difficulty being happy. Certain ones gave off an aura of stifled possibility: Lockie Alexander limping along with his polio sticks; Harry Phipps with his sunny charm, dying young of a drug overdose; the stoic little Gordon boys, whose mother had died in childbirth. The stories of my father's friends who had been killed in the war, or of Nick Tiffany who had jumped into an empty swimming pool, or of cousin Bayard Elkins, crushed to death in a motorcycle accident, evoked ancient grief.

Nothing was ever said, of course. Still, I tried to understand. I feasted on those stories of past indiscretions, old wounds, accidents and acrimonies, but I watched these harmless, graceful people, friends and cousins of my parents, cavort and play and pretend everything was "just fine." What would happen to me, I wondered: Would I be anything more than a bride in a gauzy veil?

All By Herself

ONE SUMMER DAY IN DARK HARBOR when I was about twelve, I heard my mother on the telephone. There was only one telephone in the house. It was in the pantry, skewered to the wall, the mouthpiece flaring like a trumpet from its small brown box. Nothing could be done without first connecting to the operator. To reach her, you twirled the handle on the side of the box. Mrs. Pendleton would answer from her house down the road in the village. "Number please," she would say, but usually you only needed to tell her whom you wanted to reach, and she would know where they were, not just their house number ("ring three"), but what they were doing and with whom. ("Mrs. Parish is at Mrs. Leonard's for bridge; Mrs. Holmquist is on the mainland with Mrs. Elkins.")

Now I listened to my mother promise my sisters and me off to an afternoon of play.

Someone named Miss Draper wanted us to meet her "little house guests" from England. On the telephone my mother called

Miss Draper Cousin Ruth, because in my family "cousin" was what you called anyone who was considered "family," even if there was no blood connection.

"You must go," my mother entreated us. "Poor Cousin Ruth, she has a houseful of children. She begged me to send you up to help entertain them. And they're just your age," she cajoled.

My preference would have been to stay home, play canasta at the breakfast table with pals from the tennis court, suck on a small, firm plum from Mr. Hatch's fruit stand, or read *Photoplay* movie magazine and listen to Isabel Bigley sing "No Other Love Have I" on the rickety gramophone by the fireplace and watch who was driving by on the main road. But my mother so rarely asked us to do anything for her, we felt the need to be dutiful. And I was curious.

Sybil, Tizzy and I walked up the big hill towards the Inn, then veered through the woods along East Shore Drive. Patches of hay-scented fern glistened as the afternoon light flickered through the dark spruce. We tore off leaves of skunk cabbage to fan ourselves. Racing each other up the slope, we tripped on snags of old tree root and sank our sneakers into soft sponges of moss and lurid yellow mushroom. At the top of the hill, where the road evened out, there were discreet driveway entrances, no signs or mailboxes. All you knew was that someone lived down the graveled drive and that it was private. The Draper cottage stood directly on the road, a rambling, three-story house of shingles and dark green shutters.

Miss Draper met us at the door. "I'm Cousin Ruth," she beamed at us. "We're not cousins, but think of me as one." I was entranced to have an actual grown-up meet us children at the door of her house, and to welcome us so effusively. We slipped past her into the narrow hallway. There was a long table with a vase of bayberry and Queen Anne's lace. In a large china bowl was the standard summer collection of stray tennis balls, a sole gardening glove, frayed dog leashes. Several wispy, big-eyed kids crept out to survey us, the intruders. I noticed immediately that they wore floppy brown sandals with no socks, not the regular Dark Harbor–style white canvas sneakers. These particular guests were the offspring of Miss Draper's English friends whom she invited to spend several weeks of the summer every year. There were also her great-nieces Pam and Susan Draper, daughters of Paul Draper, the famous tap dancer and, more important to me, a friend of my father's. He had recently been blacklisted as a Communist Party adherent, and Miss Draper's first concern was to care for his family.

Which was brighter, her smile or her shining dark eyes? I felt drawn to her—her shirtwaist dress that floated above her ankles, her single strand of pearls, and the way she called everyone "my friend." "This is my friend Timothy; this is my friend Rosemary." I felt warmed, intrigued.

But who were these little English brats with their piercingly clear way of speaking? "Oh what a pity," they chirped, "Anthony has to go to the loo." Cousin Ruth drifted away. We began to play abruptly, wildly, successfully. While playing Sardines in a Box, someone got forgotten in the laundry basket and tears threatened. Cousin Ruth proposed reading aloud from *The Wind in the Willows*. She seemed genuinely delighted by the story, by the afternoon's events, by our very visit. "Tell your dear mother to let you come any time soon again," she called after us when we said good-bye. "What jerks," muttered Sybil as we trudged home. "Such funny clothes," she sniffed, and we began to imitate their high-pitched accents. But secretly, I knew I wanted to return to that adventure of a house.

I had been introduced to that restless swell of energy, to the exhilarating tempo of a typical day in Cousin Ruth's summer regime. Years later someone showed me her list of "Things to Do" for her young visitors to Dark Harbor. Written in her own hand on her "Dark Harbor, Maine" stationery, it cited as worthwhile occupations: "Croquet, cards, picking balsam for pillows … rowing, canoe, sail, walk to the village for mail and paper, get books at the library and *return them*, pick raspberries and black berries, learn a poem, dance, remember your manners, [and last] go to bed!!!" Those small tasks and pleasures were familiar to those of us enmeshed in the rhythm of Dark Harbor days. Ruth Draper knew exactly what each entailed and exalted them as moments of high ritual.

Cousin Ruth seemed determined to include our family in her own. She often invited my parents for dinner (though my mother insisted it was because she liked my father to mix martinis for her guests), just as she included us sisters in her swimming parties on her stretch of beach. "Beach" is a special term in island parlance. It means an expanse of stone and pebble, lying flat along the water's edge. Each beach is marked by special stones. I can still recognize the round eggs of granite from Lime Island, the smooth fragments like hearts, encircled with a white vein deemed "lucky," from Saddle. They are imprinted on my memory like the shape of my own hand.

Cousin Ruth's beach was a curving strand of grey stone, bordered by weathered mounds of shale. After we swam in the icy water, lurching unsteadily on the uneven rocky surface in our special swimming sneakers, gasping for breath in the shock of cold and salt, we lay on those rocks to warm ourselves. Later we played "the design game" which some resourceful mother had invented years ago to while away picnic hours. It meant wandering off on your own to find things with which to make designs— sticks of driftwood twisted in gaunt, odd shapes; sea glass, which was a special prize, like a jewel in its milky light; periwinkles still oozing with life; a pair of blue mussel shells, fraily linked. Tufts of grey-green lichen, peels of birch bark, and black nests of dried seaweed became summer garlands, dollhouses, Christmas trees. Once the Gray sisters, the prettiest girls on the island, stretched out their long legs, and with the tip of a razor shell wrote island boys' names on their golden-tanned skin. They lay back on the rocks in the sun for us all to admire them.

Sometimes Cousin Ruth asked us back to her house for lunch. We trudged single-file past the bayberry hedge, avoiding the bees humming around the rosa rugosa, up the steep slope, dragging our towels behind us, limping in raggedy swimming shoes, our hair in flat wet coils, dripping down our backs. Later, transformed with brushed hair and laced shoes, and seated around her dining room table, I watched as the stone-faced island ladies in white uniform served us platters of roast lamb, garden vegetables, melon and ice cream. I find these menus in my old

Ruth Draper with Gaetano Salvemini, c. 1950
Courtesy of the New York Historical Society

diaries neatly transcribed in my schoolgirl print, along with un-
revealing entries. "We swam, we played, we ate." Nowhere do I
say what I felt, what I was thinking as I pressed close to Cousin
Ruth after lunch when once again she read to us from *The Wind
in the Willows.* I was spellbound by Ruth Draper. Amidst her
disparate bits of family I was never really sure who was who, but

I was seduced by the overflowing house, the talk of "abroad," the courtly file of foreign visitors, the sense, like the list of "things to do," of order and activity.

The first time I saw Cousin Ruth on the stage came as a surprise. Without asking us, one morning my mother announced that we sisters were to go that night with Agnes, the cook up from Boston for the summer, to Ruth Draper's performance. Mr. Hale would come after early supper to pick us up. Lester Hale's taxi was the only means of public transport on the island. His father had run the livery service that had arranged for the horse and carriage to meet my grandmother Jay at the old ferry landing thirty years before. That night we ran out of the house, party-dress sashes tied, sweaters held by one button trailing off our bony shoulders. I turned back to see my parents, thrown in relief by the dim lamplight, still sitting in the living room with their drinks and their silence.

The entertainment took place at the Community Hall, the only place of public gathering in Dark Harbor. The hall was a big upright box on the main road, where in the winter town meetings were conducted, Election Day votes cast, and the school basketball games played. In the summer, the Ladies Sewing Circle of the First Baptist Church put up tabletops on sawhorses and held a bazaar featuring the mounds of potholders, mittens, quilted blanket covers, and hot-water-bottle covers they had sewn, knitted or crocheted during the past winter. Miss Draper's performance was also a benefit for the church. It was not her church, of course; she went, like most summer people, to Christ Church, the gloomy Episcopal church on the Dark Harbor end of Islesboro. Still, she liked to help island causes. "They asked me again this year and of course I couldn't refuse," I heard her telling her friend Miss Tone at lunch one day.

Refuse to do what, I wondered? The hall was filling up with other children and other people's maids. The maids sat together, hands in laps, smoothing out the one good dress they had brought to the island for the summer as the rest of the time they were in uniform—pink or blue-striped seersucker dresses with white piqué trim.

Sybil and I pressed to the front. We fancied being in plays ourselves. I had been Prometheus chained to a papier–mâché rock in the fourth grade, and she had been Iphegenia in *Iphegenia in Aulis*. What would Cousin Ruth do that was so special? Our mother had said she did "monologues," which we knew meant she would be alone, "sort of like talking to herself aloud," explained Sybil loftily. Agnes the cook told us that she had seen her before and that Miss Draper performed "all by herself."

Someone began to flash the lights on and off. We scrambled to our metal chairs, chatter subsiding. The dusty curtains jerked slowly open, to reveal a stage bare but for a cane-back chaise longue, which looked distinctly like something borrowed from a Dark Harbor living room. Suddenly, there was Cousin Ruth, gliding quietly out onto the rickety platform. She moved gracefully, but she seemed slightly shy or embarrassed, as though she couldn't quite look us, her old friends, in the eye. She held her head down, giving slight nods of acknowledgment to the smattering of applause that greeted her. She wore a plain, long brown evening dress, holding the edge of the skirt in the gesture of the curtsy we little girls had been taught to make. "Thank you for coming," she murmured, settling herself in the chaise longue, and beginning to drape herself in a bit of pink fluff, like the bed jackets Grandma Kinnicutt used to wear. She picked up a book, leant back in her seat and let the room grow still.

Then Cousin Ruth began to talk. Her voice, always low and firm and eager, began to rise to an alarming trill. "Come in, Signorina," she commanded. We turned to watch the wings to see who would be "Signorina." No one appeared, but Ruth kept on talking to her. "Oh Signorina, I can't tell you how excited I am—to think we have arrived at Dante at last! … I'm really very proud." Gradually the point of the story began to emerge. Here this woman, definitely not Cousin Ruth anymore, but a woman rather like the dowager ladies who sat on the porch of the Inn, was having a lesson in Italian. She was reading from a book that she held but kept putting down to answer a telephone. The book turns out to be none other than Dante's *Divine Comedy*, a challenge to be sure, but it turns out this elegant lady has always kept up with her Italian, so, as she tells Signorina, "I think we are going to *skim* right through it!"

Many interruptions occurred to challenge her concentration. But she persisted with her Italian lesson because, as she insisted, "I care more for this than anything I do." Invisible as they were, we met her children who raced in with the new puppy, the manicurist, and the social secretary. We grew accustomed to the constant presence of the ringing telephone.

The children fiddled with the desk ornaments and shoved a high-back chair to scale a corner bookcase; a baby crawled into a wastepaper basket. There was a cook, Jane, who had lost her favorite recipe but would try to surprise her mistress for dinner that night. "Let's have clear soup—put something amusing in it … then we might have that fish soufflé that I like … it's white and fluffy and easy to eat … It isn't fish? I always thought it was fish—it tastes like fish, it looks like fish." Jane was replaced by Mademoiselle, the nanny, who stood awaiting orders for the day. "You see, Mad-eh-mazelle, it's rather complicated about this afternoon …" I could see Mademoiselle, plain as day, with the same resigned expression on her face that Angel's nurse wore.

When Cousin Ruth raised her arm to turn the page of her book, the ruffles of her peignoir fell back to reveal her own evening dress underneath. But the familiar persona of Ruth Draper, our island friend, had melted imperceptibly away. Riveted to this unseen bedroom of Madame, I was caught up in the life of this woman taking an Italian lesson. She lived, like so many people I knew, in New York City, with the Plaza Hotel around the corner and her car waiting outside to take her to a funeral. "What? Whose funeral? Poor old Daisy's—wasn't it sad?"

My sisters and I had often pretended to be someone else, making up stories about people we knew or wished we knew. Now, here was an adult, a grown-up who was doing the same thing.

Cousin Ruth paid attention. After lunch with her one day (just the very fact that she asked us, my sisters and me alone, without our parents, was momentous in itself), she walked with us to the porch where we had left our bathing sneakers to dry. Tizzy sat on a bench and, with her tongue between her teeth, painstakingly ran the water soaked laces through the sneaker holes.

"Just look at the way that child uses her hands," mused Miss Draper, half to herself.

A little stab of jealousy ran through me. Why hadn't she noticed something clever that I'd done? Why hadn't she said something complimentary about me? The point was that I hadn't moved, spoken, gestured in some specific way that caught her attention. She was watching all the time, probably without even noticing that she was doing so.

As much as almost all of Ruth Draper's characters intrigued me, it was the lady in *The Italian Lesson* who affected me the most. She was silly, but she was alive and animated. Sneakily, guiltily, even as a young child, I knew it was more fun for a grown-up to be out with a friend hearing some good gossip than stuck at home with tiresome children and a bored governess. And one last thing, important for a child: she had secrets.

As she disappeared behind a screen to change her clothes for her attendance at the funeral of her old friend Daisy ("everything black, Marie," she instructed her maid), she was still talking to her secretary, tossing clothes over the back of the screen. Again the phone rang. "Just a minute please," she spoke curtly into the telephone, beginning to dismiss her attendants. Her posture drooped slightly. When she was finally alone, she cradled the phone to her ear tenderly, sinking back onto the chaise, her eyes and voice glowing. "Hellooo," she cooed. It was someone important, but she didn't talk long because she was rushing to a funeral. How did I know with great certainty that on the other end of the phone was a lover? Because it must be kept a secret.

So many things those summers in Dark Harbor were

secret—elegant Ellen Fife passing out in our living room, the island men smuggling rum, my father and Aunt Ibbie sneaking away from dull formal dinners.

As a child on Islesboro, one bumped into certain surprises far more easily than in winter life with the strict regime of school routine. We, old and young, island and summer people, were all mixed up together in this tiny place. We had been coexisting here for generations. We knew each other from many comings and goings, picnics and tennis matches, Sunday sermons, sailing races and golf tournaments, deaths and marriages. One knew one's neighbor's past, who had originally been married to whom, who had loved whom in a long-ago romance, who had lost all his money, who drank too much.

Yet, as the lady in Ruth Draper's *The Italian Lesson* reminded her daughter, "We don't say such things—even when we think them, we don't say them."

Nothing untoward or shocking was ever said outright. Growing up in Islesboro I moved cautiously, edging around certain immutable facts, somehow sensing which rocks to avoid in the fog. Into all this obfuscation and adult conspiracy burst Cousin Ruth, a woman of authority who had made her own way in the world. She had been performing as a monologist for over forty years, an international success, playing singlehandedly to overwhelming critical and popular acclaim.

But of course none of this story did I know then, those summers when we played with her great-nieces and swam naked off her rocks.

Ruth Draper performed once every summer in Dark Harbor

and for that decade of the fifties I ecstatically saw each performance. The last time I saw her perform was on Broadway in New York City. Trips to New York—with its special allure and glamour—were treats and as we grew older they occurred more frequently, often after Christmas, with our mother in charge. For her, it was returning home.

For us sisters, every aspect of the visit was an adventure. First was the train from Back Bay station in Boston, clacking its way past slices of the frozen ponds and harbors of the Connecticut seacoast. China and glass rattled in the dining car; grizzled porters hovered over us while our mother suavely handed out dollar bills. We stayed in Aunt Theo's commodious apartment on East 79th Street. The doorman remembered us and tipped his hat. We never went to museums. What mattered was the theater and the shops.

Once on New Year's Eve we were to go to a Broadway theater to see Ruth perform—very kind of my mother, as I knew Ruth Draper on stage rather bored her.

"It's just that I've seen her so many times," she murmured. But she instinctively knew it was important for Sybil and me to see our idol on the big stage of New York City.

That afternoon we went to Saks Fifth Avenue. There my mother focused entirely on the heady experience of department store post-Christmas sales. She sat patiently while Sybil and I waded through racks of crumpled dresses. In the end she encouraged each of us to choose vanity over practicality. For Sybil it was a black velvet evening coat with tiny black silk knots of buttons that ran straight down the front from her collarbone to below the knee (then the fashionable length). At fourteen I had started dancing school, so I chose a red taffeta dress with a skirt that spread out like a fan when you twirled around—something I practiced doing in front of the mirror. My mother then told us the story of going to the theater as a child and being shocked when the chorus girls twirled their skirts, for then you could see their underpants. She never considered anything for herself to buy or even try on that afternoon—the point was her daughters' pleasure.

That night in the theater I felt I was in an expanded world—it was a recognizable scene of theater life, but here everything was bigger: the dark arc of space, the plush seats, the buzz of the audience. And when Ruth Draper came out on stage she too seemed bigger—not physically, but she was bolder, confident, and fully in charge. She included one piece she never did in Dark Harbor in the dusty hall with the placid maids and the restless children. It was *Three Women and Mr. Clifford*, the story of a successful businessman as seen by his eagerly solicitous secretary, his imperious wife, and finally the devoted mistress.

Afterwards my mother, always the trooper, suggested we go backstage to pay our respects to Cousin Ruth. She rushed forward from a little crush of other admirers to greet us. She trilled out in that affected, stagey voice I knew irritated my mother, "How lovely of you to come; how sweet the girls look. Do you want a lift? I have a chauffeur. We can all go home together."

I longed for my mother to accept this offer. New Year's Eve celebrations were about to explode in Times Square; we all knew outside in the cold there would be a fierce jam of crowds.

I glanced pleadingly at my mother. But she smiled politely, "No Cousin Ruth, we will be fine. We don't want to trouble you. I can manage." And she, in her ever-capable way, did, maneuvering us through the rowdy clamor, safely back to East 79th Street. After all, in New York City, she was at home.

Sadly for me, Ruth Draper died soon afterwards, in 1956. It was again at Christmastime when she was performing to sold-out audiences. That night she was driven home alone, went to bed, and never woke up. The next night the lights of Broadway were dimmed. On that New Year's Eve in 1954 as I watched Cousin Ruth on stage, my ideas of power and authority changed. Ruth Draper was in command, performing alone on the stage. I had never known any grown woman of my world to do anything so conspicuously notable before. We had our female teachers certainly, and our kindly pediatrician was also a woman, though her gruff voice and plain face were faintly perplexing to me. But here was someone my sisters and I knew, someone who came to the house, someone who invited us to hers, someone who was closer to my grandmother's age, with her long skirts and pearls, who was behaving as we young sisters did, dressing up, pretending she was someone else.

Amidst stolid Dark Harbor grande dames, the louche young men, and my own tentative mother, Ruth Draper sang a siren song to me. Which was more compelling, the fact that she lived in a large, well-ordered house full of friends, flowers and games but with no children of her own? That she sailed her own little boat by herself alone out into the bay? Or that she was an actress and had another life? She bubbled with possibilities, which I left unheeded until many years later when she floated up into my memory as the first woman I had ever known who was on her own, happy all by herself.

French Lessons

When I was nine years old I went to France with my family. We were following an aunt who had followed a man. It was 1950, the summer of the Korean War, and on the steamer crossing there was much anxious talk among the grown-ups, but we were thrifty Yankees who had bought our tickets and we were going to go, no matter what. Our pilgrimage was to France, but our purpose was to flock around pretty Kitty, the youngest of the brood, an eager young colt who, at age twenty-one, had fled the family pasture for Paris. She was in love with a man who officially posed as a member of the U.S. Foreign Service in France but who really was a member of the CIA. Once there, she promptly married her ardent suitor, Bob Bacon, and settled into an exotic-sounding Parisian life.

Her letters home, which Gran read aloud at teatime gave the menus of memorable meals or made us wide-eyed over her descriptions of swish Paris balls for which she borrowed evening dresses from fancy couture houses like Schiaparelli. Kitty wowed

*Sybil and I with our aunt Kitty Jay, Lull Brook Farm,
Windsor, Vermont, c. 1948*

the haughty French with her fresh American joie de vivre—until
the night her dress was just a little too tight and split down the
middle, revealing a dirty grey girdle. We sisters leaned over the
tea table, shuddering with delight and embarrassment.

But no one in our family ever really left home. Inevitably Kitty
was soon pregnant, produced a daughter and fell into miserable
homesickness for her mother, her sisters and even us, her adoring
nieces. So on we came—my grandmother, who had the money
and had rented the house; my mother, because she would run the
house and be the linchpin of all activities, problems, crises, just
as she was at home; we three sisters, because we were always

moved together like a bundle for the parcel post, and my father, who had plans of his own, but liked being attended to by this seraglio of women.

Gran had rented a house outside the fishing village of Honfleur in Normandy. The house Chalet de Vasouy was named grandly but it actually was a plain timbered structure. From the glassed-in porch at the back of the three-story house one could see the harbor of Le Havre, with the ships and tugboats inching their way to port. Nearby were the beaches of Omaha, still stark and dangerous with warnings of minefields, and the bombed ruins of the cathedral towns of Caen and Bayeux. History was palpable, yet at Chalet de Vasouy daily life closely resembled what we had known at Gran's in America. There was an overgrown garden, an assorted variety of dogs, the same provocative hum of grown-ups' arrivals and leave-takings. The family gathered for meals, went out during the day for drives, walks, excursions, returned at the end of the day for drinks, meals, cards, charades sometimes, but always talk, endless talk, as we gathered around the long dining room table or sat in the back room watching the boats beat their way into harbor.

A lot of the talk was about food—what we were eating, what we might eat, where we could find what we wanted to eat. Food had taken over our lives. Food to us had always been frozen vegetables and a roast. Now it became dominant, serious and sensuous. It astonishes me that just five summers after the end of World War II there was food to be had by us mere tourists, but it seemed every day that Louise the cook trudged off to the village with her limp string bag and every day we sat down to amazing meals. We were now a larger group, as it seemed every itinerant cousin, in-law, aunt or uncle had heard that my grandmother had taken a house in France by the sea that summer.

Sometimes we would be ten or twelve in the narrow, high-ceilinged dining room for meals prepared by the fierce Louise. She had come from Paris to be with my grandmother for the summer. It was nip-and-tuck if she would stay. The faint line of dark hair above her upper lip curved down in a perpetual scowl. She told us stories about Paris during the war and about having nothing to eat. "Les Boches," she'd snarl, and my mother had no need to translate. She brought her young son, Jean-Pierre, a spindly boy in short pants with pale sticks of legs. "Le père est mort," she hissed, and we girls circled Jean-Pierre in curious sympathy. But he was far more interested in sketching dirty pictures in our newly bought *cahiers* than mourning his father. Louise was in a permanent state of dissatisfaction, frequently threatening to quit because we were so "nombreuses," a state I began to associate with the full bellies of the naked stick figures Jean-Pierre liked to draw.

My genial, undemanding grandmother tried to order the simplest of menus, but Louise responded with consistent masterpieces: sprigs of green beans, crème caramel, whole perfect melons so small everyone was served their own. Louise took the plainest of ingredients—sardines from a tin, hard-boiled eggs —and arranged them so that on a platter with slices of tomato and black olives, they became a painting. She taught us to lift the spine of a sole, a gleaming skeleton, up and out from its buttery bed of flesh. Like riding a bicycle, it was a trick I never forgot.

*Sybil and I in FPK's Willys Jeepster, Omaha Beach in background,
Normandy, summer 1950*

Life centered on the daily, but it also seemed to stretch back, far and deep. In town by the port we trailed our mother on her round of errands, buying the bread, sniffing the meat, pinching the fruit. There were stories of life during the war, of hiding Allied soldiers, smuggling messages. My father gamely asked the parish priest whether the Communist Party "coupe beaucoup de glâce," in France? Uncle Bob teased my father about his fractured French, for my father came from the generation where to "cut a lot of ice" meant, in today's parlance, being in the "cool crowd." Still, one sensed the tension between the dark woes of the war and newly unstable times.

When our parents took us to Omaha Beach, a silence fell over the grown-ups as we stared bleakly across the water at burned out Nazi bunkers and troop ships left bereft on the horizon. From this same coast, William the Norman king had set off across the channel to conquer the Anglo-Saxons. My mother had read us the story of William the Conqueror and his battle with King Harold in 1066. In a Bayeux museum we filed solemnly past the long ribbon of tapestry that Queen Mathilde, William's wife, and her ladies had stitched so patiently as they waited for their men to return from war. With a 100-franc note as large and rumpled as a dinner napkin, I bought a paper reproduction of the famous tapestry. Folded-in accordion pleats gradually revealed horses, knights in armor, crude boats bouncing over wiggles of water to England. This is the way I had learned about war in school. It was as something epic and ceremonious; something different from the bombed-out houses of Caen with strips of wallpaper blowing forlornly from a window frame. Queen Mathilde was making order out of chaos, a habit I instinctively acquired during the solitary hours I spent poring over my paper souvenir, as I lay on the floor in the living room of Chalet de Vasouy.

On our return to the chalet from our visit to the Norman coast, it seemed the web and weave of contented family life was falling apart. First my father left. Not forever, not angrily; but clearly he was off on a spree. He drove away in his spiffy black convertible, a Willys Jeepster that so closely resembled the American Army jeep that the village school children recognized it as a symbol of their beloved GIs and followed my father down the road, crying "Chjeep, Chjeep."

When my father breezed back into our lives a few weeks later, he told us he had been to Spain, to a place called Pamplona to watch the bullfights. He brought out a flat leather pouch that could be filled with wine and then held up high to your face so you could squeeze out a trickle of wine. In my primness, running with the bulls seemed silly, but I deemed it even sillier to let wine run over your face when you could be sitting in a proper café, watching the world go by. Yet I also knew my father could never stay too long with the grown-ups. My mother did not interfere. She let him wander away from the very order and routine the rest of us so eagerly let her impose.

Just as in Cambridge, my mother constructed a fortress of domesticity. My grandmother hadn't a clue, having been raised with that proverbial silver spoon in her mouth. Aunt Kitty and Cousin Nancy, who had arrived with their husbands and brand-new babies, were enmeshed with diapers and feeding schedules. The only photograph of my mother during that whole long three-month holiday is of her squinting into the July sun, holding a bag of clothespins. Still, there was a sense of disturbance in the grown-ups' lives.

Everyone seemed to be crying in a corner over the fluttering blue paper of an aerogram, or sneaking off to the closet room where the telephone was lodged. Lucette, the pink-cheeked maid, ran away with her sailor boyfriend. Her mother called my grandmother to protest lax American standards. With a French/English dictionary in her lap, Gran wrote back to defend herself and her household. Kitty and Bob left for their bedroom after lunch, holding hands, while Cousin Nancy sulked in the living room in short shorts, painting her toenails different shades of red. Her husband, Eddie, insisted on reading aloud from *Ivanhoe*

My mother with clothespins, Honfleur, 1950

to us children. Sir Walter Scott bored us. We were more taken with the diagrams of how to breast-feed that we had found in Kitty's dog-eared copy of Dr. Spock. The two young married couples oozed sexy libidos even as they roughhoused with us on the lawn. When Bob was called back to Paris, Sybil explained archly, "Kitty is sad."

Why, I wondered, when she could play horses and double solitaire with us?

Upstairs in the bathrooms were small white tubs that matched nothing I had ever seen before in bathrooms at home. "It's not a toilet," murmured my mother. But she was far from explaining any connection between a bidet and babies.

When my father came back from Spain, besides wineskins he also brought some friends: Mr. Crews, who appeared with not one but two girlfriends. The girls were lean and brown. They laughed a lot and I watched their white teeth over red mouths. At lunch they picked over Louise's tiny, garden-fresh peas with long, pointed fingernails.

FPK in Pamplona, 1950

After our summer in France, nothing would ever seem simple again. Life there was the trick of peeling a peach in one long silky strip or easing a cork out of a bottle. It was butter without salt, wine at every meal, men in berets kissing one another on each cheek. I felt there was much to learn. Life was mysterious, complicated. It was like the drink I watched the fishermen mix in the harbor café, the bitter Pernod my father insisted he liked. The glass arrived on a small tray, neat and clear, but you added water and it turned yellow and cloudy.

How I Learned

It was in France that I was brought out of the figurative schoolroom, with its strict ideas of what was supposed to be, into an acknowledgment of life and its infinite possibilities, its fluid transformations, its surprises.

Gran used to say of traveling friends or family, "Are they abroad?" In my mind I pictured the ocean—broad, of course, and filled with tiny specks of people like the stiff little soldiers of Queen Mathilde. Now, I realized, I was abroad, abroad from myself and all that I had known and thought I understood.

I wonder how I learned anything.

The more I think about it, the hazier grow my recollections of any kind of ethical standards, any inculcation of moral values I received from my parents, let alone anyone else. Of course I grew up knowing it was wrong to kill (except the "Boches" and the "Japs," as they were described), and not to steal (though there was a ritual shoplifting in Woolworth's five-and-dime store with its ensuing climax of fear, triumph and relief when no siren went off and no policeman followed us home). In school we knew we mustn't cheat, though my eyes would wander over to Nancy Riddick's perfect columns of multiplication tables as I tried to nudge my pencil to emulate hers. (Was that a 1 or a 7?)

Rules, though, what to do and what not to do, what to say and what not to say, even what to wear, were a dominating bass note of my childhood.

Stand up when an older person comes into the room; shake hands; look the stranger in the eye ("if you tell me the color of her eyes, I will give you a dime," was how a friend was raised). "Never read a novel in the morning" had been the message for my grandmother, and that has somehow hung over my sense of propriety. Pay your bills by the tenth of the month, but bread-and butter letters should not be written too promptly, because then it would look as though you hadn't properly reflected on what a nice visit you had had.

There was the phrase batted around our houseful of sisters, "make an effort." This meant smile, don't sulk, stand up straight, push your bangs out of your eyes, and then, as we grew older, it meant you should turn to the man next to you at dinner and ask with great interest, "Are you here for long?"

There were lots of rules about appearance. These prolifer-ated fast, bouncing around from the bedroom to the bathroom when we brushed our hair (fifty strokes) every night.

Dress was like armour. When someone in your family died you wore a black armband and didn't go to parties except in black or grey. A hat was required everywhere and always, for my mother, and in church for us little girls. Your hat and your handbag should always match, and patent leather was considered cheap, on a par with chewing gum on the street. At the Inn in Dark Harbor each summer, someone from England came to sell kilts and Fair Isle sweaters for schoolgirls to wear during the winter. I longed to dress that way, but no one we knew in sensible left-wing Cambridge would be caught dead in such regalia.

Makeup was a minefield. No red nail polish unless it was flawless; "the minute it chips, take it off," ordered a cousin who lived in Paris and should know. It was bad to wash your hair more than once a week because frequent washings diminished the natural oils in one's scalp. (When Mary Martin came to town in *South Pacific* and washed her hair every day, sometimes twice, onstage, we learned that actresses could get away with anything. My mother's hairdresser had a friend who worked in the salon where Mary Martin herself had appeared one historic day. "It's a miracle," he said. "Her hair still has shine!") Worst of all was dyeing your hair. "A peroxide blonde" was practically a whore. Rouge hinted at promiscuity. Pierced ears meant you were foreign and lower class. Maybe a gypsy.

So if makeup was evil and no one ever discussed how much we all lied to each other ("Yes, I'm fine. No, nothing is wrong. We're all just tired. Least said, soonest mended"—again and again that refrain rang through our childhood), how did I grow up knowing anything about morals and ethics? Am I even to be considered moral and ethical?

What I am glad I did pick up from my parents *in* bits and pieces *from* bits and pieces is being on time; making a habit of looking at pictures in museums, in galleries, in other people's houses; doing what you say you will do; and always having a book to rescue you wherever you are—in your bag when you ride the bus or by your bed in the middle of the night.

But I wonder what I ever really learned in school. Growing up, my sisters and I went to a happily progressive, joyfully liberal school in Cambridge called Shady Hill. It had been started at the turn of the twentieth century by the wife of a Harvard professor on her front porch. She wanted her own children to study outside and to love books as much as they loved animals. For me school was a treat. Learning was something so easy, so exciting, so pleasurable compared to the complex business of living.

At Shady Hill our school year was organized around the theme of a "Central Subject." Each grade zeroed in on some epic period in world history. First-graders studied the ancient, honorable life of the American Indian; when you were ten and in Mrs. Dudley's fifth grade, there were the discoveries with Leif "the Lucky" Erikson, Marco Polo and Magellan. In between we actually did pick up adequate practical knowledge of fractions, cursive script (which meant how grown-ups thought of handwriting) and folk-dancing.

Most memorable of all was the fourth grade when we moved to Olympus and read the *Iliad* and the *Odyssey*. We each were encouraged to choose the name of a Greek god for ourselves. The boys mainly wanted to be Ajax or Poseidon; no one ever quite had the arrogance to grab the name Zeus outright for himself, and we girls knew it was a drag to be bossy, misunderstood Hera. For us early, unaware feminists, it was Artemis and Athena who held their sway. Artemis was much admired because she was so cool and competent, so self-reliant, with the moon as her companion and a quiver full of arrows to keep her many suitors in line. Still, in dry, academic Cambridge we all felt it was important to be a brain like Athena, even if you emerged from the head of your father. No one could imagine the airy beauty of Aphrodite who sprang from the sea. Gran had a St. Bernard named Hebe, but I knew I didn't want to be a mere cup-bearer. I felt drawn to Arachne because as she spun her web, she was condemned to silent watching. And there was something about Persephone that seemed a kinship, something about being torn between two powerful forces—the safe, embracing mother and the alluring drama of the underworld.

My proudest moment was winning the role of Prometheus in the class play. It was certainly not typecasting. No one could be further away from daring and risk-taking and audacious imagination. I clung tight to the home front, a true goody-goody in lace-up brown oxfords when everyone else wore penny loafers. But some vestige of ego moved me. Secretly at home I memorized page upon page of Aeschylus, for we peformed in translation from the original. When the pre-ordained leading man, Lexie Hawthorne, a transplant from England with a precise, piercing accent, came down with the flu, I was draped in a muslin "kiton" and chained to a rock constructed from masses of wet, congealed newspaper. I was onstage the entire time while various classmates stumped back and forth before me. Emmy Martin, the best athlete in the class, was cast as the eagle, sent from Zeus to peck and claw at my insides. But she kept a respectable distance, as I intoned woodenly out into the audience of dozing parents.

It was the first time I heard the word "transgression."

Life in Cambridge practically demanded that you transgress the norm. The eccentric individual was the hero. Cambridge was different from Boston. Mrs. Tudor, our elderly neighbor who lived across the street in a stately Georgian house, liked to tell stories of life as a child when her family would row in from Boston across the Charles River to spend summers on Larch Road. But we learned that once one was physically situated in Cambridge, its ambience stood for life outside the box and the prescribed way of conducting oneself.

Still, Cambridge, for all its emphasis on the life of the mind, the "simple" way of doing things, was a kind of cocoon—a cocoon of grandeur. Our Larch Road house was relatively modest with its small bedrooms and shady backyard. However, there were, to my child's eye, some wonderfully imposing houses. Certainly Mrs. Tudor's big white-clapboard magnificence and across the parkway of Fresh Pond, very near our street, was a nineteenth-century residence so grand it had a name all to itself: Elmwood. It was set back amidst so many sheltering trees, one could only glimpse its widow's walk and its neighboring barn.

Farther away on Brattle Street was the poet Henry Wadsworth Longfellow's house, cheerfully yellow, wide-windowed and open to the public on certain afternoons. His granddaughters, the Misses Thorp, taught at our school and we learned to recite from "The Children's Hour," about "laughing Allegra, grave Alice and Edith with the golden hair."

Down in the bustle of Harvard Square was Harvard Yard itself, where my father went to work every morning. The Yard was a kind of sanctuary of green lawn and brick formality. You walked through impossibly high wrought-iron gates to enter, leaving behind the temptations of St. Clair's, where Gran took us for underdone English muffins, or Arlace's, where we bought new shoes every fall before school started. Once inside the Yard, one could wander unnoticed amid students tramping by with bookbags slung over their shoulders, and grey-haired professors pushing dilapidated-looking bicycles. All these places, redolent of splendid isolation, meant amplitude and prosperity for me.

—⁂—

A starker reminder of living life outside the norm was the shadowy presence of the "displaced persons," as we were taught in school to call them. At Shady Hill there were several adminis- trative types who spoke with accents, who dressed in just slightly different ways from the usual down-at-the-heel Cambridge out- fit. Most Shady Hill parents dressed to look poor; these women in their worn cardigans and sensible shoes really were poor.

"What does 'D.P.' mean?" I asked my mother.

She quickly shushed me. "It means they are refugees, from the war in Europe," she explained. "They have had terrible lives and you must never say 'D.P.'"

So these women with foreign-sounding names at school, or those who worked at our favorite Viennese pastry shop in the Square who wrapped up delicate, star-like sugar cookies in brown paper boxes, became in my imagination more gaunt, more bent, more heroic tragic figures than I had previously perceived them.

If they did not belong here, I figured neither did I. I myself vaguely felt the outsider; in Cambridge we were considered "rich"; in Dark Harbor we were "poor." We lived in Cambridge but we weren't true Harvard intellectuals. My parents went to parties in Boston and there were those cousins on the North Shore. It was unsettling a bit, not to really belong anywhere, but I also liked identifying with the outsider.

Cambridge stood for something. What it was, was not quite clear, but I felt it subtlely around me. On the Cambridge Common was a rusty marker, "Here during the winter of 1776–77 camped the soldiers of the Continental Army." High on the wall of Christ Church where Sybil and I sang off-key in the children's Sunday choir was a plaque certifying George Washington had worshipped here. I could recite by heart "Paul Revere's Ride," or at least the first four lines; that very date was a state holiday. Gradually I gleaned that life in Cambridge stood for speaking up, making yourself heard, no matter how controversial.

Protest was important. Our second-grade class was asked to refrain from using the afternoon privileges at the Mount Auburn Skating Club because someone had detected that our group included a young black child. Instantly the class mothers insisted that the whole school boycott the club. The club's admission policy changed soon afterwards.

By 1954 I was studying the American Civil War, spouting William Lloyd Garrison, "I will not equivocate ... I will be heard," a new and interesting word. The Army-McCarthy hearings were underway in Washington and shown almost daily on television. Both my parents were riveted, even breaking their rule of "no television" and renting one just for the hearings.

I prepare to graduate from Shady Hill School, Cambridge, 1955

Joseph Welch, the courtly Boston lawyer in his polka-dot tie, became our hero. But bravest of all, to me, was my gentle mother, amidst the frenzy of rigid, liberal Cambridge, explaining that, charming and cultivated as Adlai Stevenson was, she would cast her vote for Eisenhower because she believed that he best could contain the dangers of McCarthyism.

I loved Shady Hill with its high-minded, unorthodox ways of teaching and learning. But at fourteen, when we ninth graders wept at "Closing Day" in June, the abyss of "what next?" loomed. I fell back on the most narrow and traditional of paths. For three years, it was I, not my parents, not social pressure, but I, who wanted to cloister myself away in a relative nunnery of a school. St. Timothy's School, for girls only, had been started after the

Civil War in the lush Green Spring Valley outside of Baltimore by two spinster sisters, Miss Sally and Miss Polly Carter, for the sole purpose of rebuilding the family fortune. My Jay aunts had gone there, and I think I imagined some of their charm would rub off on me. Maybe I wanted to fit into the box.

There was nothing scholarly about the Carter sisters. They only wanted to save their beloved house, Redlands, back in Virginia from the ravages of the postwar depression, and there was nothing scholarly about St. Timothy's. I had fallen from Olympus. Timothy, besides being a man and a saint—two things I had no interest in being—was a weak vessel, a straight man for the bold importunings of St. Paul. "O Timothy, my good and faithful servant," we recited sleepily at morning prayer, and I felt doomed.

But it was my choice and I endured it. What we learned at "St. Tim's," as we called it, was how to be men. Rich, successful, white, Anglo-Saxon men. There was an emphasis on not showing your feelings and following many, many rules. Rules dictated how not only we, but also our rooms, our closets and bureau drawers, should look. Every morning there was a room inspection, with the names of the offenders read out at breakfast. There were rules about when to write letters and when to wash our hair. There were rules about when to go to bed at night and when to get up in the morning.

We wore uniforms that were comfortingly unbecoming. But no matter what getup was required, we were constantly expected to change it. In the fall and spring during the morning we wore tunics with bloomers that buttoned at the side. In the winter we climbed into midcalf grey flannel skirts with a choice of either grey (dark) or blue (navy) sweaters. At night for dinner, teal-blue scratchy wool dresses and thick lisle stockings were prescribed, but with warm weather we hurried into pastel shirtwaists. On Sunday, when we went to church twice in the day we were allowed "free choice," which meant cashmere sweaters and pearls, neither of which I owned, or camel hair polo coats, which I also didn't own. I had a thin grey duffle coat in which I awkwardly stood out, but I wore it like a hair shirt because I didn't want my parents to have to spend any more money on this expensive, unnecessary school.

We were instructed in lots of games (from which I fled by inventing many sore throats, cramps, headaches, so that my only exercise was walking the lane that led from the discreet entrance gate to the imposing stone manor house where we all lived). There was also much emphasis on grammar and something called "Current Events," which entailed subscribing to *Time* magazine and which would give us something to talk about with our future husbands. Marriage and the future were on everyone's minds. Outside the study hall was a large bulletin board studded with clippings from the *New York Herald Tribune* society page as to which recent graduate was engaged to be married. Then, when she actually was married, a large photograph was displayed and everyone would gather around to critique her dress, her veil, the way she had done her hair.

We were taught to think of others, especially the needy, the poor, the downtrodden. Somehow it was decided that what would help the needy, the poor and the downtrodden the most

My father and me at graduation from St. Timothy's School,
Stevenson, Maryland, 1958

was our own handiwork. When news reached the school of the brave Hungarian freedom fighters battling the Soviet tanks in 1956, we each were required to knit one square of fuzzy, grey wool that would eventually be turned into a substantial blanket for some luckless but stalwart patriot.

And every Sunday afternoon during Lent the entire school gathered to sew baby clothes for unwed mothers. We sat in small circles of straight-back chairs; no one was to speak; as a treat,

Miss Watkins, the headmistress, would read aloud to us from one of John Marquand's Mr. Moto mysteries.

The only thing I remember learning was the term *basso continuo*. Mr. Gottshalk was the music history teacher who trudged in from the Peabody Conservatory in Baltimore. He had pop-eyes and played the harpsichord. He introduced me to Bach's Brandenburg concertos. As he explained, "There is something that never changes, that is always present and that is the lower line of the composition. It is called the *basso continuo* and you must listen for it. When you hear it playing, then you will know this is classical Baroque music." Perhaps that is why I chose this strange, unfriendly school. After the disturbances of home and the exotica of Shady Hill's Olympus, I was seeking something that never changed, that was always the same.

If Shady Hill represented the airy life of ideas and imagination, and St. Timothy's emphasized the practical and the worldly, my college learning is a haze. As my college I chose, or rather was chosen by, Radcliffe, part of my beloved Cambridge, yet separate and distinct. I felt I had been anointed when I was accepted into that august company. Unfortunately I do not remember one single thing that was imparted to me in any class by any professor. I wonder if anyone ever did bother to teach me or even reach me on any level in college. The trouble is that I went to a college dominated by men. What mattered was what they knew, what they remembered—their concerns, passions, and ambitions. I was boy-crazy so I was only too happy to oblige. My eager, vaguely intellectual self picked up a different scent at college. Training, discipline, curiosity were put on hold. Now agreeable,

Party girl, 1961

accommodating manners and a pleasing countenance mattered.

Almost immediately my whole value system changed. Going to college was a release. I began to do as I pleased. Suddenly good grades, studying hard, memorizing into the night was not the only thing I cared about. During that freshman year in ugly, new-brick Comstock Hall, I developed an unspoken competition with another girl on my floor. The contest centered around who

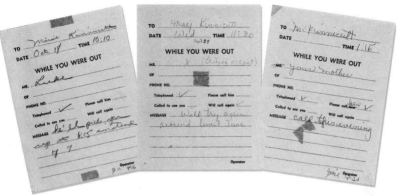

"While You Were Out" notes, 1958

garnered more "Mr. X" slips. When the girl on "bells" answered the telephone downstairs at the central desk, she would fill in a form recording who had called. It was considered dashing of the caller not to leave his name. The important fact for us incarcerated female students was that it was a man, a mysterious foreign entity, Mr. X himself, who had been trying to reach us. We never really tried to figure out who Mr. X was. We only knew he was someone from "down there," in Harvard Yard where the freshmen lived, or better yet, from the mock-Georgian buildings along the Charles River where the upperclassmen lodged. My head was definitely turned. I had been noticed; that was what counted. I would do anything—anything decorous that is—for male attention and approval.

When an upper classman asked me to a matinée in Boston, but told me he wouldn't be caught dead seen picking up a mere

"Cliffie" (considered dreary by cool Harvard upperclassmen), I walked to the Square so as not to in any way embarrass him. When another friend and I were asked to have dinner with two debonair *Harvard Crimson* editors, it did not bother us that we spent most of the evening coloring their Modern European History maps, due the next day. Our own work was suspended, only too happily. What mattered was that we were having dinner, such as it was, with two dazzlers, and that they would take us dancing at the Palace afterwards, a questionable dance hall in the seedy side of Boston. And most impressive of all, as we had to "sign out" in a large register when we left the dormitory, everyone back on campus hopefully knew where we were, "fallen women" in some out-of-bounds locale.

One was accepted as a student at Radcliffe on the grounds of academic distinction. Many of the women in my class were brilliant and are now professors, judges, authors and analysts, lawyers and doctors. One even ran for mayor of New York. But a small group of us didn't want to be thought smart or brainy, we only wanted to be deemed attractive, desirable and popular.

Harvard boys squirreled away in their dorms, reading the Freshman Register, which included a photograph of every Radcliffe undergraduate as she entered college. They held a contest, voting for the prettiest girl in the incoming class. Her reward was the title Miss Radcliffe. The year I was a freshman, the competition was banned by some perspicacious dean. I was disappointed, I longed even to be considered a member of the rejected aspirants. "Too bad," joked a friend of my father's, "I guess they broke the bra."

In my studies, cursory at best, I also sought male approbation. When I met my tutor, it did not seem odd to me that his quarters were so small that I had to sit on the edge of his bed while he lounged in his leather chair, critiquing my work. As an American history and literature major, I was required to submit a suitable topic for my senior honors thesis.

"Why don't you do William Gilmore Simms. No one has ever tried that before and you might even get it published," my bored tutor languorously suggested. Say no more, I was off to the library. It never occurred to me that I might have found a more appropriate and interesting subject than an eighteenth-century Southern male writer, yet clearly I was dragging my feet because five months later I still hadn't gotten past page one of Simms' first novel. As I sobbed on Observatory Hill to George, my current boyfriend, he asked me, "But Maisie, what do you want to write about?" I pulled back from my snuffles, and reached down into a part of my childhood memory. "Edith Wharton," I stammered.

In those days at Harvard, declaring an interest in Edith Wharton was similar to researching Danielle Steel nowadays, but for me it was a natural flow of family history. It was as though she were part of my family. I had grown up with the tales of my great-grandfather, Dr. Kinnicutt, physician first to Wharton's mother, then to her husband, who was odd and took to eating his meals under the table. In my mind's eye, I had pictured beautiful, unhappy Countess Ellen Olenska from *The Age of Innocence* as looking like my beautiful, unhappy Aunt Theo. So I wrote my thesis on the New York novels of Edith Wharton,

Engaged at 21 in 1962

entitling it "The Dark Spectator" because I was drawn to the figures of diffident observers like Newland Archer and Ralph Marvell. Was it that they reminded me of people in my own family? I hammered out my paper in the hot flush of another new romance, which ended in my being engaged the night of my twenty-first birthday.

When I went to meet my professors as part of the required oral defense of my lamely brief thesis, one of them asked me, "Do you see the dark spectator as a precursor of post–Civil War malaise?" But the examination hardly mattered. Word filtered back that on seeing a shiny diamond flashing on my left hand, the professors had lost interest in my academic prospects. I was in the grips, all too happily, of the male hegemony. My boyfriend that stormy night on Observatory Hill had given me permission to pursue the unorthodox, but I still ended my college years with the traditional seal of approval, an engagement ring.

And yes, now I do remember one thing, one loose phrase from my college learning. In looking over the obituary page several years ago I saw that a Professor Kenneth Lynn had recently died after a distinguished career at Johns Hopkins. In 1960 at Harvard he had taught a class on Mark Twain. As an American history and lit major, I was required to take his class. If nothing else I was an assiduous note taker. Professor Lynn, smoothly blond and polished, was given to pithy aphorisms. I sat in the front row, eager to catch his eye, writing down every clever word he uttered. Then it came. He was speaking of Huck and Tom on the raft together, of their great friendship and how that bond would change each of them forever. "Love and freedom are incompatible," pronounced Professor Lynn, and I dutifully wrote the words down, thinking what nonsense, of course you can have both love and freedom at the same time all the time. In short order, out of the blue, I was to learn how wrong I was.

Death in the Family

The day before he died, my father asked me to come home for dinner. Family suppers with my mother and sisters were evenings he had never much cared about. Still, he did ask me to come back to Larch Road that night. I had begun to resist doing what was expected of me. I was on my own now, at college. Even though my dormitory was only a few miles away from the quiet street where I had grown up, I had worked out a pleasant, quasi-independent life for myself. At Radcliffe I forgot about trying to be on the dean's list, and relished boyfriends, late-night parties, Pete Seeger concerts, Bach oratorios, avant-garde theater. I knew someone who knew someone who was in Timothy Leary's nefarious graduate seminar. He reportedly gave out Seconals to help devotees calm down after taking Benzedrine for exam all-nighters. I came home to have my mother do my laundry and cut my hair. I took mincing little steps towards being "different," exotic. I raided the attic and hung my bedroom with leftover curtains from my grandparents' house that sagged over the dusty floor of Saville House, the so-called off-campus lodging for older students with supposed sophistication (even though nervous graduate students watched over us as "house mothers" and the college rule was still to be back in the house by 1 a.m.). I splurged on Arpège to squirt in my bathwater. Over my mother's doubts, I wore her best black coat to the weekly Saturday afternoon football game. It wasn't the overt borrowing; it was that "no one wears black to a football game." Of course I was far from radical. I have always known how to play both sides of the street. I am not the middle child for nothing.

When my father asked me to come home for dinner that January night in 1961, I hesitated. "I have exams, it's midterms, I must study," I pleaded, suddenly the serious student.

"You can study at home," he persisted. "You can study all night right here at home if you want. I just think it would be nice to see you. Come for half an hour."

I had always resented his own cameo appearances at family evenings, but that night I relented. I have never liked to say no, even when I am thinking it.

I went home to the grey frame house on the street that was named for the larches that had once grown there in groves. I sat in my old bedroom at my upright brown desk with its cluster of cubbyholes and the secret drawer where I hid the five-dollar bills my uncle sent me at Christmas. I gazed out the window by my desk and watched the blue-violet shadows of a winter afternoon deepen across the crusty snow of the backyard. I stared bleakly at Professor Schlesinger's *The Age of Jackson*. I underlined "the business community has invariably brought national affairs to a state of crisis and exasperated the rest of society …" and then it was time to go downstairs to the dining room with its red curtains drawn against the night.

At supper I told my father that the businessman is the enemy of the liberal tradition. My father, who made fun of people like his own father who were businessmen, laughed and threw his napkin at me. "Don't get stuffy in your old age," he teased.

After the table was cleared, he was suddenly tired. He wanted to go to bed, but he also wanted my mother to cut his hair. That ritual was one of the few times I ever saw my parents in any kind of physical proximity. They would come upon each other unexpectedly in the same house at odd moments during the day, but they hurried past each other as though stung by mild electric shock, heads down, eyes averted. Yet my father preferred that my mother cut the thin grey hair that framed his hawk-like, green-eyed face. That night he sat up in bed while she crept carefully around him, clipping away at his balding head with long steel scissors.

I stood in the doorway to say good-night: to cross the room to kiss him seemed too much of a gesture of surrender. "Aren't you glad you came home?" he glowed with a parent's way of being right.

I could hardly wait to leave. I escaped eagerly, to return to my college house in time for a quick gossip before sneaking out for a beer at Cronin's. The night was cold and I kissed my boyfriend fast on the steps of Saville House.

The next morning was my American nineteenth-century history exam. I was ill-prepared. The blank pages of the blue examination book loomed alarmingly. A slight shiver of dread ran through me but I shrugged it off. I knew then that the supposed "study" at home had been a mistake. I knew I would have been better off in the cosy library of Radcliffe Yard, slyly watching who was sitting with whom. Harvard men could come up from the Square to study with us, but we could not go down to study with them at their library. But what mattered now was hurrying through these questions, which now seemed to mean nothing to me; I could barely grasp the sense of what I was trying to say. At noon I had to be at Professor Guerard's Contemporary English Lit class. Everyone who took this advanced course was older and extremely good-looking. After the inconvenient interruption of midterms, I yearned to be among these lofty graduate students. I shamefacedly handed in my blue examination book, for I knew I had done poorly, but then tripped merrily along the icy sidewalks, hugging to myself my Christmas-present yellow coat.

In Emerson Hall Professor Guerard stood up before the chattering throng. He also was handsome in a steely, grey-haired way. We rustled quickly to our seats.

He held up his hand to silence us.

"Before we begin I'd like to speak to Miss Kinnicutt. Would she please come forward?" His impassive face searched the crowded hall.

Now this is fun, I vainly thought. Now everyone will see me in my new coat. I swished to the front of the room.

Professor Guerard's eyes gravely locked with mine. "You are to go home immediately."

"Why, what have I done? I don't understand?" I stuttered. Why can't I stay here with you, I thought wildly.

He only sternly repeated, as though I was particularly dense, "You are to go home, now."

To reach Larch Road, if you have time you walk along stately, tranquil Brattle Street, picking your way over brick sidewalks, stubbled bumpy with the roots of ancient elm trees. You can also take the trolley car that rattles past the Mount Auburn cemetery near our house. That day I ran into a taxi, simultaneously willing it to go faster, then wishing it to take me far away. I leaned forward giving directions to the unconcerned driver, sweating in my yellow coat.

Springing up the front steps, I saw through the side window into the dining room where another hawk-headed man with his back to me was standing, a telephone at his ear. He looked like my father.

"Dear God, don't let it be Mummy," I prayed. The front door swung open.

My mother stepped forward; she had been watching for me. I stared at her hard. She was here; nothing else mattered.

She spoke haltingly, "It's Daddy."

I thrust myself before her, daring her to tell me the truth. "Is he dead?" "Yes," she nodded, and relief flooded my frozen heart.

I stumbled into an oddly familiar living room where my uncles, my father's brother and their Uncle Bayard, encircled me. They told me my father had died instantly that morning of a heart attack. He had just reached his office in the Boston Juvenile Court where he worked part-time as a pro bono probation officer. After he left Harvard due to poor health (and probably with little desire for a full-time job), he had still wanted to work with young, lively people, no matter how recalcitrant. One of his colleagues had told my uncles that my father dropped dead as he was consoling the mother of one of his wayward clients. She could barely speak English but afterwards she apparently kept repeating, "what a nice man, what a nice man." My uncles seemed comforted by this story and so was I, though later I couldn't help but feel it was the old tale of the shoemaker's children having no shoes. All his life, everyone was glad to see my father except maybe his own wary, dazzled family.

In an amazingly brief passage of time, the ice-cold blow of the moment began to wear off. Our house that had seemed so tense and prickly began to fill with people, extra unknown family, next-door neighbors, far-flung friends. Everyone expressed shock, for my father was only fifty-two. They arrived somber, teary, heads down as they shook snow from their boots, but soon everyone was kissing, embracing us, telling us how much our father loved us.

Really? I wondered. But I warmed to the situation, the attention, the platters of food people kept bringing. The dishes of deviled eggs and creamed lobster were like party food, for that's what the day was turning into. Stories circulated about what an amusing, eccentric character Frankie Kinnicutt was, how he stood up for the underdog, how he wasn't afraid to tell certain pompous types they were "pour les oiseaux," his favorite phrase of opprobrium, meaning in 1920s slang, ridiculous, dismissible, literally "for the birds."

It impressed me that these lively, affectionate people I had previously avoided at family gatherings were suddenly there in our living room, sitting beside me, patting my hand, confiding in me. "We were in school together. He was my oldest friend, even though he went on to Harvard and I gave Yale a run."

"He taught me about China," one eager youngish woman buzzed in my ear. China, I puzzled, he loved pretty things, but china...?

"Red China," she hissed triumphantly. "He said we should recognize it."

Around four o'clock that afternoon Aunt Theo took me in her car to stock up on tonic water and ice for all the drinks that were being splashed down. She was not a confident driver and I had a shaky sense of direction myself, so we rambled about Cambridge, weaving back and forth on the Parkway for a long time.

"Poor Maisie," she sighed as we finally drew up in front of Larch Road with our groceries in hand. "This will probably be the longest day of your life until the day your own husband dies."

I drew back, reflecting. A husband? I had long been a bride in my fantasies. But would I really be married someday?

That day was a Friday. On Monday there was to be a memorial service. I dreaded Monday because I knew we would be expected to cry. For the first time ever I would have to see my mother cry. My father's sister instructed my mother how to behave. "In our family we always walk down the aisle behind the coffin."

"There isn't going to be any coffin," my mother snapped back. "Frankie wanted to be cremated."

My aunt shrank away. "No mourning either?" she quavered. At

my grandmother Kinnicutt's funeral my father had worn a dull black armband; my mother wore a veil and the darkest of suits. After six months she eased into beige or white dresses for parties, but no color for a year.

"Where does she think I'm going to find a veil now?" muttered my mother under her breath. "I don't want to wear color because I feel sad," my mother explained to my sisters and me, "but you can wear whatever you like." I wore a blue wool dress and splurged at the hairdresser because I hoped friends would be there to notice me in my new grief. Later, trying to be nice, Aunt Gusty told me I looked like a stewardess.

The memorial service took place at Christ Church in Cambridge, whose door my father had hardly ever darkened except to wave proudly at Sybil and me in our children's choir appearances on Christmas Eve. That Monday afternoon after the service, my mother and sisters and I all crawled onto my parents' bed. That in itself was unusual, as we were often reprimanded for rumpling its immense, lifeless surface. My mother eased back against the pillows. Tizzy nestled protectively by her side. Sybil brought up a tray of tea and cinnamon toast, a favorite treat. I sat at the end of the bed, holding my mother's narrow, bony foot in my hand.

"Let me rub your feet, Mummy." I knew she loved having her feet massaged. I would almost cut my finger on the sharp edge of her bunion. "No." She shook her head, edging herself back up against the pillows. "I must get up." But then she sank back again, giving in to intimacy, to repose, to restful moments for which she had had so little time.

Watery sunlight washed over the pink luster of the teacups on the bed and warmed the tight buds of the forsythia in a vase, clipped from a backyard bush. Outside, icicles dripped peacefully from the eaves. The flickering light made me blink. A hesitating tear slid down my nose. I sniffed at it in one relieved gulp.

"Read us some of the letters you've gotten," I suggested, for I suddenly wanted, not for my father to be there, but to be able to mourn him freely, unrestrainedly.

"There isn't much time, we have to be at the Peabodys' for dinner," she automatically demurred after so many years of keeping her emotions in check. "But here's one that's rather sweet from Cousin Harry."

"Dear Aunt Sybil," she began. "I once sailed with Uncle Frankie from Newburyport to Rockland. We got lost in the fog at Small Point. All we had to eat was raisins and brandy." Her voice started to break, but then she caught herself.

"Poor Frankie, he always was terrible on a boat," my mother smiled. She shook her head at the very memory, and we all let go in laughter.

It was the beginning of the first lesson of a loving life, a trick my genial father had never quite mastered on his own family turf. I'm sure he knew, he just never said it. I was learning it is possible to love someone and tell him so at the same time.

Ten years later I return to Dark Harbor. I have a nice husband, two nice children. We have rented a cousin's house for a month. I am curious to experience life on Islesboro as a grown-up.

Aunt Ibbie invites me to dinner. Ibbie was, as ever, Daddy's cohort in Dark Harbor, allied in the powerful, slightly sexy intimacy of cousins. Aunt Ibbie makes me feel as shy and awkward as she did when I was twelve. I have never felt comfortable with her rapier wit.

Tonight Aunt Ibbie and I are alone. My husband is the businessman I scoffed at in my Radcliffe years. He works hard and comes to Dark Harbor only on weekends. The children are at home with the aupair. After dinner, as I am about to leave, almost to hold me back, Ibbie says, "Your father was my best friend. I adored him. I think of him almost every day since the day he died."

I am embarrassed by such hyperbole. I say nothing in response and stare out into the velvet night. In the harbor a bell buoy rings clear; the slack ropes of the skiffs slap against the dock.

I carefully thank Aunt Ibbie and, just as carefully, slide into my car. Driving home, it is dark and thick with fog but I wheel easily along familiar roads: up the Holmquist driveway to the main road, past the Catholic church, left onto Ferry Road.

In our rented house the children are asleep, played out by the high jinks of a Dark Harbor summer day. The aupair girl is locked in the harsh glare of the television. I slip into my room without turning on any lights. Leaning against the door, I hold myself, hugging my arms to my ribs, and begin to cry. I cry in deep, painful, satisfying gasps. I am finally weeping for my father, the man I really never knew—nor did he know me—but of whom I too think of almost every day since the day he died.

Who Would Have Thought

On the morning of the day I was married, I treated myself to a long bath in the big tub in the pale green tiled bathroom of my childhood. I thought, something momentous is happening, but am I part of it?

"Who would have thought," as my grandmother liked to say about fortuitous but unlikely events. It was 1962, the year after my father died, the year I was to graduate from college. It was also less than twenty years after Gusty's wedding, when I had pressed my face close up to hers and Huffy's at the tea table topped by the wedding cake, in joyful anticipation of marriage and the happiness it intended.

Joyful anticipation was not precisely what I felt as I lay in the cavernous tub. Here I was in the bathroom of my coming-of-age. The bathroom with the ivory-yellow sink with its long crack in the bottom covered over with graying adhesive tape, where on dancing-school days my mother used to soothe me by washing my hair. She would add vinegar to the second rinse, "to make it shine," because we both knew I had to be perfect for dancing school. Later, as a clothes-crazy teenager, I soaked my newest treasure, nylon stockings, in this sink, and then left them as wet snakes to dry from the towel bar. I sometimes shaved my legs propped up over this abyss, blotting the nicks with scraps of toilet paper.

Now I was scared. I had met Jamie Houghton, the man I was to marry, only a year before, a few months after my father had died. We had decided we loved each other enough to spend the rest of our lives together, forever and ever, until death us do part, a vow that Gardiner Day, the minister of Christ Church, had—a few weeks before—casually referred to in his study on Farwell Place.

"It's not to say you can't get a divorce. There are problems in marriage," he intoned, rifling through the scattered papers on his crowded desk, not looking at us, in a hurry to get away. Yet it was part of his pastoral duty to offer this marital counseling before he actually faced us, all of us beaming and sweaty, at the altar.

"Three problems exactly: sex, money and in-laws. Do you have any problem with any of those?" he asked, still not looking directly at us. "No, no," we shook our heads soberly. Kissing and necking and loving Jamie was fun and easy. There seemed to be plenty of money floating around, and I had only met the Houghtons once. Mrs. Houghton had telephoned my mother to say she thought I was "charming," so surely that wasn't an issue, and, of course, Jamie adored my mother. I only had a problem with being happy.

It wasn't that I didn't love Jamie. He was hard not to love. Darkly handsome with thick black hair slicked back on his bold head like an Argentinian polo player, he had an eagle's beaked nose and a radiant smile. Practically everyone felt drawn to Jamie.

Gran pronounced immediately that she liked him. She told my mother she liked the way his hair grew in a neat point at the back of his neck (because, of course, that was the way her own children's hair grew). When Aunt Ibbie met Jamie she eyed him up and down. "Well I must say you're not what I expected," she said. "I imagined you'd be large and fat and blond. In fact you look rather like one of our family." Both sides of the family, Kinnicutt and Jay, believed that to look like one of them, dark and slim and bright-eyed, was the ultimate compliment.

Was I marrying my brother? A look-alike? People in Jamie's family said I looked like his sister, not the sexiest comparison, but we did seem to share a certain affinity, a certain shared emphasis on presentability and cautious, eager straining to be liked, to have people think well of us.

Our initial meeting had been inauspicious. Though it was under circumstances similar to my own parents, in that it was inevitable that we should meet, still for Jamie and me, it was an evening of accidents.

A suave upper class man at the Harvard Law School, always a province of sophistication in my mind, had asked me to dinner. "The Comédie-Française is in town," he promised. "We'll take in the play, go back to my place for supper and champagne afterwards."

No matter that I was already going to the very same Molière production the night before with someone else, and that my French was minimal, and that I was vaguely in love with several other elusive people, I still accepted Harry's invitation. I was flattered and curious.

The evening of the performance the girl on bells telephoned my third-floor room. "Someone is here for you," she announced. I tripped downstairs to face an imposingly well-dressed, unknown presence, someone who seemed too grand, too perfectly groomed for the dim hall of Saville House.

"Where is Harry?" I asked crisply, vexed at being kept waiting, at any slight change in my calendar.

"In the car, with Lisa," said this large, calm person. My mind reeled. Harry must be foisting me off on this stranger. And indeed as I walked out to Harry's Thunderbird, there Lisa was ensconced in the front seat. Her dress à la Chinoise was slit up the side, her blond hair gleamed under the streetlight. Worst of all, she had been a few years younger than I at St. Tim's. Now she was the star, the prize of the evening while I was extraneous, a mere blind date. In my four years at Radcliffe I had never been on a blind date. There was practically a waiting list for people who wanted to take out Radcliffe girls. Humiliated, afraid that someone might discover I was on a blind date, I sulked all the way into Boston. Six months later I was engaged to this proverbial tall, dark stranger, Jamie Houghton.

It helped that my sisters took to Jamie right from the start. Instinctively he knew to woo them as he was wooing me. After the first noncommittal introductions on my part, Jamie would bound into the living room of Larch Road with presents—a bottle of Pouilly-Fuissé for Mummy, Everly Brothers records for Tizzy, kisses for everyone. "He reminds me of a beetle," insisted Sybil, home for a visit, glowing with the worldliness of New York City. "Bright and black and shiny."

Jamie definitely did have a kind of shine, a shine that came from being always loved. He insisted, in our confiding walks along the Charles, that he was as anxious as the next guy, but still he exuded a kind of faith, if not precisely in himself, in life itself.

He also had the buffed polish of being rich, and being comfortably unapologetic about it. All my life I had been drifting around the periphery of rich people, uncertain as to just what having money meant. My grandmother's house on Long Island with its faded grandeur cast a romantic glow on the stories of coming-out parties and chauffeurs who served as gardeners in a pinch. Yet all that money had disappeared, thanks to bad luck and carelessness. Dark Harbor was a bastion of rich people even if my family wasn't, but in Dark Harbor everyone who had money seemed unhappy. Another mixed message came from growing up in Cambridge, where having money, particularly going out and making it, was privately looked down upon.

I never would have married Jamie if my father had been alive. Daddy was jealous of rich people. They had things like big houses and fancy cars that he made fun of but which he also wanted for himself. Except that his big house, his smart car would be nicer, chicer, and peppier than theirs. Daddy knew he could make fun of rich people but he also knew he didn't have the energy or the guts to work hard enough to make money of his own.

Jamie blew into my life after the death of my father, and my confused image of rich people expanded. Here was somebody who came from a family who lived as well or better than anyone in my brush with Long Island life, who had as much money as anyone in Dark Harbor but who was happy, lively and productive. He was the fifth generation of a family-owned glass business in upstate New York, where his father and his brothers seemed to be working hard, and loving it to boot.

I relished having a boyfriend who could take me to the Ritz bar every night if I wanted, who wore cashmere sweaters as a matter of course, who stocked up on any book that caught his fancy (no waiting for the public library here). But I was equally enchanted by the idea of someone who approached life and its privileges, the very pleasure of living well, with such gusto and enthusiasm.

Jamie was finishing up at the Harvard Business School when we met. Four years older than I, he had already been in the army, had already worked two years on Wall Street counting bonds in the back room at Goldman Sachs, and he could hardly wait to begin working for his family business, not because his father expected it of him but because he wanted to and thought it would be, in his words, "a lot of fun."

Having fun and being rich and working hard were acts of daring I struggled to embrace. I was so used to tucking my head down, being cautious, wearing Sybil's hand-me-downs, putting clear nail polish on my stockings to catch the runs, waiting my turn for a new novel at the lending library of the Personal Book

Shop in the Square. On hearing that Jamie and I were engaged, Lena, the stalwart French-Canadian who had been coming to help my mother at dinner parties ever since we were children, announced triumphantly, "Maisie always was the smart one."

I didn't feel smart during those first months of falling in love with a rich man. I felt appalled. What was I doing with someone studying, not particularly arduously but diligently enough, at the Business School? In all my years in Cambridge, I had never even been to the Business School. It wasn't even really in Cambridge as far as I was concerned.

Still, the afternoons on the banks of the Charles, the dinners in out-of-the-way French restaurants, then somewhat of a novelty in Boston and Cambridge, the sheer surprise of being with someone so alive despite his three-piece suits, so decent despite his affinity for Republican politics, who danced the two-step, who hummed in my ear "This could be the start of something big" and asked the band to play that song at any party we went to together, who was so in love, not only with me, but with life in general, became ultimately, irreversibly seductive.

On the eve of my twenty-first birthday Jamie asked me to marry him, but I still wasn't sure. He invited me home to Corning and we stayed in the big brick house his grandfather had built. It was called The Knoll, a name which appeared in red letters on neat stacks of stationery in every bedroom, but principally on pads of paper in the room called "the telephone room."

A maid whisked my suitcase away to unpack my things and to press not only my dress for dinner that night, but also my nylon stockings. Jamie's mother met us in the high-ceilinged library where John Law, the longtime butler—almost a family member, though remote and disdainful in his uniform of dark jacket and striped trousers—carried in the tea tray. I knew I was being inspected and was so shy I couldn't think of what to say except to ask what "knoll" meant. "Isn't it a valley?" I stuttered. "No, dear, it's a hill," Mrs. Houghton murmured politely.

That night at dinner Mr. Houghton appeared in a red velvet smoking jacket and John (by now in tails!) passed another tray at the end of the roast beef meal. This time it was cigars and cigarettes laid out on a silver platter. The flame of the torch-like lighter attached to the tray was already lit, so one only had to slightly nod in the direction of the lighter to start one's smoke. Mrs. Houghton took one puff of her cigarette, then crushed it out on one of the Steuben glass ashtrays in front of each place. I said, "No, thank you." I had never been able to breathe out and smile at the same time.

On a hill we indeed were, with the town spread below us and the broad Chemung River curling through. There were factories by the river, billowing smoke and blowing whistles. The next day Jamie took me down to a plant where television bulbs were made. The sight of the huge black globes lurching off the assembly line, the glare of the furnaces, was like an epiphany for me. "This is power," I thought, and decided that I would marry Jamie after all.

This momentous decision occurred in January. We were to be married in June, a few weeks after I was to trail into Sanders Theater in rented cap and gown for my Radcliffe graduation. In March my dutiful mother, a widow at forty-seven who dreaded giving parties and meeting new people, who had never heard of Corning or the Glass Works and who had never laid eyes on any of Jamie's family, announced she would give us an engagement party.

The equally dutiful Houghtons with their large extended family of in-laws, maiden sisters and numerous grandchildren agreed to attend. My mother roped in a few friends who actually knew of Corning and its Glass Works and who assured her the Houghtons were very nice. Which they indeed were, it was just that there were so many of them and they accepted this invitation to a "small party" with such alacrity.

The afternoon of the gathering, I came home early from classes supposedly to "help." This entailed bursting into tears and telling my mother I thought I had acted too hastily, that perhaps I wasn't ready to be married to Jamie. At that moment of breakdown my mother had been wedging the vacuum under the big yellow Davenport sofa, the sofa we sisters threw ourselves on when we wanted to neck with our boyfriends.

She set down the hose, carefully winding the extension cord into tidy coils, and drew me down onto the sofa. "There's absolutely no need for you to go through with this. We can cancel this party right now if you like." She waited calmly.

Snuffling noisily, I glanced around the room, fresh and pretty with the bunches of anenome she treated herself to for special occasions. In the kitchen, I knew, were buckets of ice, glistening rows of borrowed glasses, cold shrimp and tiny codfish cakes ordered from the Somerset Club. Upstairs was the snappiest outfit I had ever owned, a black and white suit from Bendel's in New

York, complete with shiny black patent-leather high heels.

"I guess we can go on with this evening," I confessed resignedly. "Then we'll see."

By the time the evening was over my mood had improved. Everyone had come, the entire Houghton clan, all my old boyfriends, looking appropriately chagrined, even Mrs. Tudor, our venerable neighbor from across the street. She cornered Jamie in the hall to tell him how much she liked the pink bubbly wine that came from his neck of the woods in New York State.

The Houghtons not only came, they came bearing gifts. At the end of the evening, I was wearing a gold bracelet studded with flower-like rubies, and on my desk sat a tiny gold clock. Even my mother was pleased. Exhausted, triumphant, she sank back on the yellow sofa, sipping a beer, her usual bedtime drink. "The Houghtons really are very nice. I thought they would be café society."

Still later when I voiced lingering doubts, as the date grew nearer, Mummy, somewhat exasperated I suspect, sent me to Dr. Dalrymple, the wise old family friend who was a psychiatrist.

"I feel haunted," I told her, referring to Duncan, a blue-eyed poet with a motorcycle, who, rather belatedly, was trying to convince me I was making a big mistake. I had loved Duncan and his extravagantly romantic letters with phrases like, "loved your moments of glad grace," until I realized he was cribbing from Yeats.

"Of course, you feel haunted," she replied. "Duncan reminds you of your father. But your father is dead now and you must go on and make your own life."

Thus it was that I lay in the bathtub that humid June day, half expectant, half frightened. I still had one more terrible act of rebellion to perform.

Even with my doubts, I was totally prepared to be a regular bride. My wedding dress was a loan from my well-to-do New York cousins, another hand-me-down just as I had always worn, but I knew their things were far nicer than anything I could afford. My sisters were my bridesmaids along with two friends from St. Tim's. The four of them, dressed in stiff yellow organza, perched on my bed as I tottered around uncertainly in too-tight, new high heels, trapped in an engulfing crinoline that propped up the frothy dress of Belgian lace.

My hair had been puffed into a tidy pouf the day before but as I went to my rickety little dressing table, I noticed that my hairbrush was missing. Suddenly my good-girl facade snapped. I stumbled out to the hall. Mummy happened to be coming up the stairs, bound on some purposeful errand in the last half-hour before my uncle showed up to drive with us to the church in the hired limousine.

"Where is my hairbrush?" I demanded crossly.

"I'm not sure, darling. Where do you think you last used it?" she asked innocently.

In a voice of command all too familiar, I shouted, "Find it, right now!" She shrugged her shoulders and moved on about her task. Who would have thought? I had become my father.

The actual wedding was a blur, not a blur now, more than forty years later, but a blur that day itself. Nothing seemed to take very long. The portentous vows at the altar raced along; guests nodded at me in the receiving line; the photographer snapped away at lightning speed. The photographs later revealed that the dainty cap sleeve of my dress was slowly ripping apart.

The only moment that seemed to last forever was when courtly Mr. Houghton, my brand-new father-in-law, asked me to dance. We edged our way onto the makeshift dance floor that had been constructed on the lawn of the newly spruced-up back-yard of 15 Larch Road. He held me respectfully at a distance, our movements hampered by the crinoline. We smiled politely as we circled the tipsily slanting floor. I eyed the distant knot of old beaux, now disloyally, cheerfully chatting away with my St. Timothy's pals. Not one of them approached us. Mr. Houghton circled the tiny patch of floor again. Still no one made a move towards us. There I was, a wallflower, stuck at my own wedding.

Suddenly I wanted to leave the scene, to quit my own party. I did not feel any part of the festivities. I fled from a baffled Mr. Houghton and extricated Jamie from a circle of old Wall Street buddies who had flown up for the weekend.

"I think we should leave soon," I announced peremptorily. "In fact, what about now?"

Somewhat startled but ever obliging, Jamie agreed and soon we were running out the door, down the steps of the familiar grey house where I had lived these past fifteen years. The wedding guests threw paper rose petals at us, I stopped contritely to embrace my mother. Whether or not I thanked her I am not sure.

Lena, resplendent in her black uniform, drew me aside.

"You be good to him," she admonished me. Lena was as wise as Dr. Dalrymple but I was too pleased with myself to notice.

Jamie and I leaving Larch Road after our wedding, 1962

I was getting my own way for the first of many times with patient Jamie and most important, I had broken the cardinal rule of Dressing Up. For my going-away costume, my shoes were orange and my handbag yellow. They did not match, nor would they ever again.

It was a short-lived victory, however. Soon I was weeping in the car as Jamie drove us towards Cape Cod, to his aunt's cottage by the sea where we were to spend our wedding night. "I miss Mummy and Sybil and Tizzy," I sobbed all the way down Route 3, to the edge of Buzzards Bay and the town of South Dartmouth.

It wasn't until we reached Aunt Libby's snug sea cottage bordered with beach rose that I began to brighten up. In fact it was her icebox that almost instantly improved my mood. Aunt Libby had clearly put a lot of effort into stocking it with every delicacy any peckish guest could desire—a whole fat pink ham, avocado salad, chocolate cake. Along with the usual gin and whiskey, a bottle of Château Margaux waited on the bar table.

"What's that?" I sniffed. "Just about the best wine there is," beamed Jamie, already grappling with the corkscrew.

Once again the Houghtons seemed to know about presents, about enjoying the moment, about what made life worthwhile.

Never Apologize, Never Explain

I WASN'T ONLY THE ONLY ONE who was being lightened by life in a broader world. Curious things began to happen to my mother also, after the death of my father.

It seemed to begin with food.

There was an odd chemistry between my mother and food. At first it appeared she didn't care. Our meals when I was growing up in Cambridge were memorable for what they lacked. No wine, no fresh vegetables (except the occasional avocado—which we called "alligator pear"—dumped in the salad bowl along with chunks of iceberg lettuce and slices of hard little hothouse tomatoes), no bread (unless you counted the triangles of dry Arnold's white toast presented with the Campbell's-soup first course). Potatoes were baked; rice was white and gummy Uncle Ben's. Macaroni-and-cheese was for "poor people."

The main meal in our house in the 1950s was a variation on a theme: steak, chicken (which we called "broilers") and hamburgers. A leg of lamb usually appeared at Sunday lunch, stuck in the oven at 300 degrees as my mother was hurrying off to church so that it was a comforting grey by the time we returned. An overcooked roast was a tradition that had started in her parents' house on Long Island in the thirties. But there the meals were served by a continuous round of maids.

Though she only had the help of a weekly cleaning woman, my mother insisted on following the prescribed form of family meals with which she had grown up. This routine began by calling Egan's market on Huron Avenue. They cheerfully delivered twice daily to the tonier sections of Cambridge. There was no question of my mother going to the market to actually see the food herself. She always wanted the same thing, so how could it be any different?

Egan's delivery service was the only luxury my mother permitted herself. In our house she was the cook, though without much appetite. At the end of the day she would be in the kitchen, tearing open packages of frozen vegetables, giving a quick polish to silver forks left too long with the breakfast egg. Around six o'clock, she changed. Dressing for dinner was a long-standing principle with her (she often reminded me that in the early days of her married life with my father, she wore an evening dress and he wore a smoking jacket, even if they were alone). At seven she took a bourbon and water into the living room where my father sat with the newspapers and a martini, excusing herself to slip back and forth to the kitchen to check on various whistling pots. She then served the three-course meal in the dining room to my father and we sisters, once we were finally allowed to join my parents at table. She later retreated to the kitchen to wash up, though she allowed herself to leave the greasiest pans to soak overnight in a puddle of Joy.

Once I came home from school and cornered my mother in the kitchen as she was sprinkling frozen French fries on the blackened and battered cookie sheet, just prior to melting Kraft cheese on top of Triscuits to be served as cocktail nibbles.

"I have to bring a recipe to school for something called a casserole," I announced. "It has to be in a dish you can pass." My mother drew back from the oven. "I don't think I've ever made a casserole," she said, puzzled. Then she rallied, asking "Would *boeuf bourguignon* do?"

—⁓—

In point of fact, my mother was good cook. She understood about butter, eggs, sherry in the black bean soup, chicken stock and cream. She was simply too busy and too unhappy to give time to anything that might be pleasurable. Dinner in the dining room with the red curtains drawn against New England chill had been a painful hour with a moody husband and three sullen schoolgirl daughters. Abruptly this unhappiness ended when my perpetually spoiled, perpetually charming father dropped dead of a heart attack that icy winter day.

At first, my mother had moved about in a haze of muffled grief and regret. Yet almost immediately, there were slight sparks of change. Flattering dresses in bright colors began to appear in my mother's closet. She traveled to Paris with a maiden aunt, and to Yugoslavia with school friends. She worked one summer in the back hills of Kentucky as a volunteer for the Frontier Nursing

My mother, Dark Harbor, 1963

Service, mainly because that expedition brought her back to her old love of horseback riding.

By this time in the mid-sixties, I was a complacent married matron living in Switzerland. It was a treat to have my mother visit. I was eager to show off my newfound domestic skills, which meant trudging off to the market every day, basket under my arm, sometimes twice a day if the milk on the door stoop was forgotten or the baguette of bread turned stale. My mother trailed after me, inspecting the fish's gills, sizing up the lemons, telling me I was brilliant to manage in my broken Swiss-German. She loved the swank Zurich restaurants and impressed the sommelier with her quick take on the wine. She knew about cheeses and pastry and which vegetable belonged with which season. "Are the strawberries from California or are they really from here?" she quizzed the waiter. I began to realize how capable she was of enjoying herself, but I was still shocked when one day she casually remarked, "I hope I marry again."

Looking back at old photographs now, I see her as I never could see her then. There she is, still not yet fifty, with thick, dark hair (discreetly colored), bright, shining eyes, a shy smile—a lanky, graceful figure with those enviable long legs. More than pretty, she was a beauty because now she was happy.

Others began to notice too.

One summer on Martha's Vineyard she rented a house with a field reaching down to the harbor where she could gather her family far away from Dark Harbor, which my father had preferred. She spoiled us all, new grandchildren, daughters, doting sons-in-law. Indulging her family was something my mother valued highly.

Every whim was catered to: her jewelry box was open house for the three-year-olds, crabmeat for lunch for the thirty-year-olds, jaunts to antique shops, picnics on South Beach, tennis doubles which she usually won for her less capable partner. So again I was surprised when she announced one evening that the next morning she would be leaving the island for the day. "I'll be back on the last ferry," she murmured, almost apologizing.

"Where are you going?" we sisters chorused, wondering how she could even contemplate leaving perfect, companionable us for the heat and traffic of the mainland.

"Someone has asked me to lunch and I'm meeting him in Barnstable."

"Oh, Mummy," cooed bold Sybil. "Do you have his picture?"

Eventually my mother married Bill Waldron, her devoted, even ardent, suitor. He was divorced (almost, and meeting my mother hurried the process along, so that later we teased my circumspect mother that she was a "home-wrecker"). A Boston lawyer, he was as steadfast as my father had been elusive. My mother settled into long-denied marital harmony. We sisters gleefully noted each sign of her freshly minted happiness: a new double bed installed in her old room, houses in Portugal rented for holidays with friends, classes in yoga and, for my once tense mother, something called Transcendental Meditation.

True to her nature as a well-trained geisha, my mother turned herself inside out for Bill and nowhere more than in the kitchen. Bill was a big man who could eat a whole box of Cheez-Its before dinner, and whose idea of heaven was pie à la mode, then more Cheez-Its. My mother set out to refine his palate. Now, there were lots of trips to special markets for just the right cut of swordfish, the ripest melon, the freshest bread. She lavished hours on meat loaf, minestrone, ham mousse, dishes she never would have considered for my father. They ate in the kitchen with candlelight and afterwards read aloud to each other from

Bill Waldron and my mother, Rensselaerville, N.Y., 1970

Trollope or Toynbee or, at the time of the Balkan crisis, Rebecca West's *Black Lamb and Grey Falcon.*

Julia Child was in her heyday—a Cambridge neighbor actually—and my mother took pride in knowing just where Julia shopped. It was the vogue to pay attention to this master of French cooking, and though my mother certainly had no desire to emulate Julia's repertoire, she admired her fearless exuberance. When I today force myself to cook for a party, I think of my mother, my mother who walked with her head tucked down, who wrote thank-you notes for thank-you notes, who started out every invitation with "I hate to bother you," proudly quoting Julia on any culinary mishap, or for perhaps just life in general, "Never apologize, never explain."

Late Bloomer

Now I am supposed to be grown-up. It took me a long time "to be myself" as my mother so exhorted me during those anxious Cambridge years. I still hum the mantra of self-belittlement, but it is an old habit, that cautious look over one's shoulder to ward off the angel of destruction. I am one of the "late bloomers," a phrase my grandmother used to describe some wayward friend who had finally "come into her own." But what is my own?

For a start, Jamie and I have actually stayed married, no matter how much I test his patience. When we were first married I screamed about everything, from where were my earrings to why was he such a stuffy, bridge-playing Republican business-man. Now I scream only about a few things, like where are my earrings and why is he still a Republican (he has given up the bridge).

We have beautiful children who now have their own equally beautiful children. Home is Corning, New York, the town whose smokestacks and factory whistle drew me out of my Cambridge complacency more than forty years ago. The smokestacks are gone, but I enjoy the calm surroundings of the Southern Tier—that often forgotten part of New York State.

But for so long I felt I had only hitched my wagon to a star, that is, to my husband and his career, and that there was no "me" there. I suffered from frequent bouts of laryngitis as though I literally was losing my voice. I spent a lot of time lying on my bed reading—Virginia Woolf, Doris Lessing, Joan Didion—but nothing sank in.

It was all part of my retreat from life, or, if not life, a retreat from living my life more freely, perhaps even selfishly. Once upon a time I imagined I would spend my days writing; that seemed the most estimable way to spend my time. Writing about what I was not sure but in my mind's eye I saw myself as a "writer." It was the first thing I wanted to do and thus the thing I always put last, deeming it a private passion to be indulged later. About thirty years later I woke up to the fact that this fantasy had not been realized—because I had not done anything about it.

It took a horrendous automobile accident to knock me to my senses. An accident not to me, but to Jamie, the activist who stepped off a sidewalk at the wrong time. As he was three months in and out of hospitals, I gave up my good-girl volunteer work to be with him. When I eventually re-emerged into my little community of Corning, I quickly saw how dispensable I was.

What I knew I wanted to do with my last days, if I were spun off a sidewalk like my poor husband, was to get back to things that had once meant a lot. It had to do with words and stories and how people live their lives. And it had to do with not always doing what was expected of me. It came over me as a visceral rush; I knew I had to start writing.

Thirty years had actually taught me something. I knew I needed the discipline imposed by an actual teacher. I enrolled in a memoir class at the West Side Y in New York, conveniently near our own apartment. There were admittedly low expectations as the class was described as being "For people who have lived and worked and want to tell their story. No experience necessary." For me, in the process of evoking family portraits, the memory of my beloved cousin Ruth Draper floated back like an amazing gift. I began to write a book about her.

On one level there seemed so much that we shared. Ruth came from an Old New York world that was so similar to my own and she was one of four sisters. She created a world of make-believe and always felt slightly the outsider. Then, of course, our paths diverged sharply. It was as though we switched roles, or switched centuries on each other. I married the respectable, achieving businessman and followed him around Europe and America while he climbed the corporate ladder. Ruth defied cultural expectations, and, though she also spent much time in Europe, it was to further her amazingly successful career in the theater. I never really did anything by myself. I was cared for and spoiled by my indulgent husband. I hired nurses, nannies, babysitters, cooks, cleaning women, decorators, landscapers, gardeners, all of whom gave me a very nice life amidst charming surroundings.

Meanwhile, Ruth Draper always went her own way, and, most important, she wrote all her own material. I decided to call the book *All By Herself*, something I had never been.

As my research developed, many people said "no"—something I wasn't used to hearing. There was a frosty encounter with the "Boswell" of Ruth Draper, Miss Dorothy Warren, someone who had been working on her own biography of Ruth for over twenty-five years. We started out pals and were like two proud parents, fondly regarding our darling, "our Ruth." But when Miss Warren sensed I was a possible rival and might upset her carefully constructed applecart, she proceeded to have me barred from the New York Historical Society, where the Draper sisters had donated an extensive archive. I had to threaten a lawsuit if I was not allowed back in to sift through the letters, journals, postcards and diaries, all held together by rusty paper clips. Miss Warren (as I insisted on calling her—still in my good-girl, curtsying mode) was the expert and I knew it. But for the first time in my life I relished fighting for something I wanted.

I had lots of fun, and did actually finish my book, but writing about Ruth was in a way another good-girl approach—the Radcliffe way: attack, research, tie up the loose ends. The reaction from the editors who actually read it was: we want to know more about the narrator.

Thus it was that Ruth Draper, master of many voices, creator of many characters, gave me my voice not only to tell her story, but also enlivened my own desire to be heard. I wrote about myself in the story of Ruth, for her life kept reminding me of my own. It was not the details or even the circumstances that were the same, but the choices and the turning points. I could have been a character in one of her pieces, she who paid attention to different aspects of a woman's development, courtship, widowhood, or of a woman seeking work or romance or independence on her own. It is as though I wormed my way under her microscope, into her vision, with her acute powers of observation, and stamped my foot, "here I am, look at me."

Thus, I now sense my own voice. But it has emerged over time. I sometimes wake myself up screaming. "What is it?" asks Jamie, alarmed, shaken from his deep, dreamless sleep. I ask myself too, what is it that is so urgent, so frightening that I must call out for help?

I never scream in public life. I am much too decorous, too discreet, too smart. But once I almost did. At a dinner party— where much of my life takes place—I sat next to a pleasant, gravelly voiced man who told me about his family, his children, their children, his move from South Africa, how much he liked the United States. There was a pause. Now, I thought, now he will ask me about myself, tell me what a good listener I am. He leaned forward confidingly. "What are your husband's outside interests?"

"Why don't you ask me about my outside interests?" I retorted icily and moved away from my seat. I had worked to keep myself in the background, but now I wanted to be seen, to be noticed, to be petted and praised. Perhaps I was remembering my mother's unspoken yearning, "Don't look at me, but tell me I'm attractive, intelligent, worthwhile."

In my dreams I often find myself in the gray-frame house of Larch Road where I lived for a mere fifteen years. I never dream of Corning or of the roomy house where I have lived for twice as long. Sometimes I am a child in that familiar house on Larch

Road and I am trying to shut the door against someone who wants to come in, to intrude upon our space. The force on the door is frightening, and I push back hard against the invader. "No, no," I cry, and then I wake up.

In other dreams my mother is there with my sisters and me. We are closing the house. It has been sold and we are dividing up the possessions. My mother is helping us decide what should go where. It is half a lovely dream of remembrance and pleasure at being with my mother again, and half a tiny nightmare of dealing once again with her gentle but firm demands—her insistence that everything be done fairly. But we have dealt with that, Mummy, no one wants the tea set, the blue water goblets, I think in the dream, and it is a relief to wake up.

I do not want to relive the past, but I cannot stop telling the same story over and over again. Am I trapped in the hall of Larch Road, forever trying to get my parents to look at each other while they brush past each other, hurrying in opposite directions?

A small grandson once spent the night with us. He woke early and I bundled him into our big bed, believing there was nothing cosier for him—or for us—than to be the child in between the two giant, warm bodies of his grandparents. He rested for a while between us, quiet and cherubic. Suddenly there was a thrust of his golden head. "Out," he cried.

I want "out" also.

"Roll back your shoulders, shake your head 'yes'" commands the exercise teacher, and I feel I could shake off these ghosts. They are there, they are always with me, but they are harmless beings, friendly and benign. Once when I was that serious child, my father asked me a hard question.

"How much do you love me?" he said. "Show me." I held out my arms, "This much."

"Only that much?" he grunted, but I resisted throwing my arms out any farther because that wouldn't be true, I couldn't let myself love him that much, it was too difficult, too difficult to love him and too difficult to show him. Now I want to show him.

Jamie and I return each year to Dark Harbor, though not to the white farmhouse in the village. That cottage has been bought and elaborately decorated. It is picture book–pretty now, though if you look hard, you can still see the slump in the middle of the roof. As I walk by, I try not to look. The house still holds so much of me. I long to go back into those rooms and find myself there, peering out from the bedroom at the head of the stairs. I am scared of not finding anything familiar, and one day when I do wangle my way in, I am startled by the cheery brightness of the house, its fresh-painted wicker furniture and gleaming exercise machines.

The house where Ruth Draper lived is also still standing and bears much the same outward appearance. Large and comfortable, it remains a loving family house with bicycles on the lawn and hammocks on the back veranda. My friend Pauline lives there now with her many children and grandchildren. I ask her one day if I might come and "soak up the atmosphere."

Someone is vacuuming around the toys and games spread across the floor, the stereo is scratching out a Beethoven symphony. I wander through the spaces I once knew and still find somehow exalted. Was this the corner where we sat as Cousin Ruth read aloud to us? Did she and the regal Miss Tone (who, I discover in my research, was, as a young woman, the private secretary to Henry Adams at the end of his life) preside over this dining room? The wide porch is, as always, an outdoor living room with deep chairs set facing the West Bay, books left in chaise longues and towels draped on the railing.

I end up on the second floor, where Pauline urges me into Ruth's bedroom, a place I never saw as a child, even when we played Sardines and were given the run of the whole house.

I feel I am trespassing. I am entering a shrine, the holy of holies, the room she crept to after parties where no one asked her to dance, the place where Ruth lay dreaming of Lauro, her lover killed in the Italian Resistance. It is a modest, slant-ceiling space, the way all Dark Harbor bedrooms once were, with the simplest of narrow beds, a painted bureau and straight-back chair. The view is what matters, out onto Brackett's Channel with the Camden Hills beyond. The evergreens, thick and dark, close in around the house. Ruth would want to attack them with a good pruning.

Vistas around the old Dark Harbor Gold Coast houses are tidily, consistently well pruned now. No house can be too big or too grand. New rich people press in on the island, buying up precious land and building immense barn-like structures with skylights and wine cellars, cast-iron eagles at the driveway entrances, lights like Christmas tree candles strung along the private docks. Everyone wants her old kitchen modernized with unused pantries knocked out to make way for all-purpose tables, and family rooms with television ("but leave the copper sink, it's perfect for flower arranging," I cry to the prosperous contractor who designs renovations on his home computer).

All life on the island seems streamlined now, like those souped-up kitchens. Little planes scoot in and out of a landing strip entitled Islesboro Municipal Airport. In the field bordering the strip, daisies and Queen Anne's lace bend to the rush of the engines. Speedboats with names like *Sassy Seal* and *Zoom* flash through Gilkie's Harbor, though the race committee sternly protests at the annual meeting of the club. People dash to the mainland for special supplies, health-grain bread and virgin green olive oil. A nice island girl who teaches at the school in the winter, and cuts lawns with her electric power mower in the summer, offers massages. Rumor has it, she might even give treatments like leg waxing and electrolysis.

Modern conveniences have come to the island. Certainly there's no need for a hand laundry like Mrs. Hale's. Sheets, socks, tennis clothes are thrown willy-nilly into the dryer. One foggy morning, I stand by the whirring washing machine with perky Myra, the island woman who comes to help with dinner parties, as she shows me Mrs. Hale's old trick of pouring boiling water over blueberry stains. We hold the tablecloth tight between us as she lifts the kettle high; we watch in delight as the inky blue spot melts into the steam.

But "the good old days" are not what I want. I am much happier now than I was as a child. I have a nice, loving husband who revels in Dark Harbor, perhaps even more than I do. Jamie is the one who belongs, with his "successful businessman" glow

(Dark Harbor has always loved rich people). He is content on his sailboat out in the bay, but when he wishes, he plays in club tournaments, and hits the golf ball straight and far. I smile to think he is my "trophy" husband, the prize I was brought up to win.

One day our son brings his fiancée to lunch. Jamie walks in as I am setting the table. "What are you doing?" he asks. I have dragged out every odd saltcellar, wine coaster, and water goblet. As I fiddle with linen napkins, dessert plates and salad forks, I think of John Law, the family butler who worked for Jamie's parents. He set the table every day with a yardstick. "What am I doing?" I ask myself as the blue day beyond beckons. Even the kitchen equipment—the flour sifter, lemon squeezers, a flint whetstone for the knives—seems archaic. "I want to show them how it's done," I explain. This is the way we do things, I think—or is it?

The loony, scatty ways of old Dark Harbor are fading away. Club life looms large. People are on committees; organization is important; calendars with the entire summer's activities plotted out in neat squares with the time of the tide and the face of the moon arrive in one's mail in early spring. There is a waiting list for new members of the Tarratine Club, and on Sunday nights people gather for a buffet of lobster tails au gratin and beef Wellington, lavishly spread out in the tiny, crooked rooms of the golf house. An elderly friend tells me she remembers overhearing Ruth Draper interview a possible cook for the summer. Club life would never have drawn Ruth. My friend listened to Miss Draper reassure the young woman, "We're fourteen at table every night and we never go out to dinner."

Pictures of beloved members who have died are on the walls of this golf house now turned smart dining room. There are photographs of my father in his sailboat, or jauntily posing with friends on an island called Tumbledown Dick, famous as a spot for especially long, boozy picnics. There were, until recently when I insisted to the House Committee, no pictures of Ruth Draper.

One summer in Dark Harbor I find boxes of correspondence my mother had saved. Maybe these are the diaries of my father's that I once stumbled upon in the Larch Road attic. Suddenly it seems a reprise of my desire to discover something, any clue, secret or not, as to what the people in my small circle were thinking.

The oldest are letters between my Kinnicutt grandparents, those pair we sisters were brought up to dismiss as cold and undemonstrative. They are quite to the contrary when I begin to read their correspondence.

The letters are postmarked "Dark Harbor, July 1906," or "Ipswich, 1907," "West 37th Street, NYC, 1909." My grandfather Gustav Hermann Kinnicutt was a young banker, working in New York City, traveling on the train every weekend back to his parents' house in Morristown, New Jersey. It was Hermann's father who was the sagacious doctor of Edith Wharton and, most importantly for me, the one who decided the fresh air of "simple" island life in Maine would do his family good.

These Kinnicutts lived in the red-and-white stucco cottage in Dark Harbor on that little point of land overlooking the fairy-tale island of Thrumcap, and it was to Dark Harbor that my grandfather Hermann wanted to entice the girl for whom I was named, droll, sassy Miss May Appleton Tuckerman. They seemed already to have fallen in love, as the letters I find speak of the wretchedness of their separation. She is stuck in Ipswich, a tranquil backwater village of Boston's North Shore. But to spend a whole, long summer in Ipswich with her history professor father up for a vacation from his teaching at Princeton and her keen-eyed mother overseeing a brood of brothers and sisters was clearly no match for the lures of racy Dark Harbor.

The letters from Dark Harbor and Ipswich fly back and forth, fervent, happy, until there appears to have been a falling-out. May has hurt Hermann, and he writes reproachfully but with that delicious humor I had always been told belonged only to my grandmother. Yet here he, the agitated lover, can clearly keep his wit as he writes, "Why haven't I heard from you? … I hate you for not writing … I hope you have a bad egg at breakfast." And he must have been an ardent pursuer because there is one fierce telegram spang in the middle of all the lovers' palaver.

"Return at once to Sunswick (the Tuckerman summer home) STOP. DO NOT PROCEED WITHOUT CHAPERONE," is the sharp directive from May's father.

But they did marry and the letters continue, less prickly, less yearning, but eager with love and happiness at the life they are building together. Home and fixing up home are their shared passions now.

"Don't forget to bring the wallpaper samples, I can't decide which curtain material is best, what do you think?"

The new bathroom is too expensive. "Why were bills ever

invented?" Hermann finds a tiger-maple bedside table while he bicycles through the New Jersey farmland and he pays six dollars.

It is the instinct of the magpie bird, feathering its nest, slowly adding the small embellishments that make home perfect, unassailable. I think of Jamie and myself tripping over the new carpet samples in our first apartment; of my grandmother Jay who couldn't live in a house that didn't have western light; of the round rosewood table with the dolphin base they bought in Paris that I have inherited from these Kinnicutt grandparents.

I find to my surprise that I have fallen in love with Grandpa and Grandma Kinnicutt, whom I always shunned in preference for joyful, indulgent Gran Jay. They are hardly the cold, sterile collectors I once imagined. They are affectionate, funny and touchingly human. He writes to his "dearest girl" from "your own boy." She replies, "I am so lucky to be in love with my husband."

I understand why my mother found them remote. By the time she arrived in the family they had shrunk from life, withdrawn into an agony of grief and bereavement. Their youngest son, my father's brother Bayard, had dropped dead of a heart attack at the age of twelve. There are boxes of condolence letters amongst the papers, but I cannot bear to open them. I grew up with "Bydie," as he was called, as the archetypal reminder of loss, and years later, as some kind of reparation to my father, I name my only daughter Nina Bayard.

But the biggest surprise in the box of letters is what they teach me about my father.

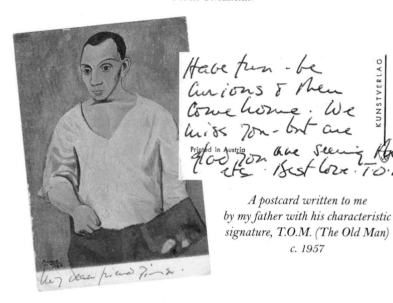

Have fun - be
curious & then
come home. We
miss you - but are
glad you are seeing things
etc. Best love. T.O.M.

*A postcard written to me
by my father with his characteristic
signature, T.O.M. (The Old Man)
c. 1957*

The cache of letters in Maine inspires me to go back to the slim packet of postcards my father sent to me when I was at St. Timothy's. I have saved them now for over fifty years, but I seldom read them. I am afraid of being too moved, too haunted. When I received these cards at school, standing outside at recess between classes, waiting for mail call, I was embarrassed. Everyone else's father, if they wrote at all, wrote on creamy sheets of embossed office stationery. The letters were about dentist appointments and train schedules for Easter vacations in Florida. My father wrote on postcards from the Museum of Modern Art or the Egyptian collection at the Museum of Fine Arts. He once chose a dissolute Degas prostitute slumped in a boulevard café and asked if "this is you and Lizzie [my best pal] discussing the past vacation?" He wrote under a Picasso self-portrait, "my dear friend."

I am stunned by how loving and parental these postcards are.
He worries that I am homesick. "I miss you already," he writes,
"but 'missing' times do pass." Another time he reassures me,
"Always there are moments when the work does not seem to go
well & all is black. This is the way of the world ... Please don't
worry though I know this is easier said than done. We will have
some fun when you come home & I will build your morale to the
soaring point. Always call home & reverse the charges."

Did these brief missives sustain me at school? I am not sure.
I had been growing hard on my father and his errant ways. I
probably deemed it typical of him that he could be so charming in such an abbreviated form of communication. These were
postcards, after all. Still, I have guarded them faithfully all these
years.

What moves me now is what my father ever so slightly revealed of himself and his private thoughts in those snippets of
correspondence. Not only was he frequenting museums and
New York galleries, but he himself was beginning to experiment
with paint, color, form, design. He pilfered stationery from the
Porcellian Club, his hangout away from Larch Road in those
Cambridge years, and began to daub the backs of miniature invitation cards with bright, fearless color. I think the small size
appealed to him, a larger canvas would have been daunting.
Repeatedly in his notes to me I find references to his desire to
paint.

"I am wildly making collages with shells and old nail files I
find on the beach."

"Doing a little painting but not with much success."

FPK painting on board his houseboat, c. 1959

"I hope I will be living happily on the boat painting master-pieces, living in the sun and acting like Picasso."

The "boat" was a houseboat he had had built in a fantasy of navigating the eastern-shore inland waterway, but it proved un-seaworthy and he kept it on the Parker River, near Newburyport, not far from the beloved Sunswick of his childhood. It was an hour's drive north from Cambridge and he went there on week-ends to entertain friends, to paint, to be alone. The houseboat became a studio for my father, complete with tiny gas burner, rocking chair and numerous needlepoint pillows embroidered for him by his lady friends. Still, my mother encouraged him in this retreat, understanding that he needed an escape from the

A page from FPK's logbook with photos of the Zuleika Dobson, *c. 1959*

cramped spaces of Larch Road, increasingly dominated by his daughters who had little patience for his vagaries.

The boat was christened *Zuleika Dobson*, after Max Beerbohm's heroine in his Edwardian satire of Oxford undergraduate life. The first time I heard the word "cynosure" it was applied to the coquette Zuleika, "a cynosure of every eye." She wore a pink pearl in one ear and a black one in the other. The pearls changed color according to how the wearer felt about the suitor to whom she was presently speaking. Now I wonder if that was how my father remembered himself as a young man, ablaze with seductive petulance.

When he first embarked on this adventure he bought himself

a nautical logbook because that is what he envisioned the boat as being, a barge on which he would travel. But as the bulky oddity became more of a miniature house and less a seaworthy boat, the log became his personal journal in which he wrote random thoughts and observations, repeated amusing stories, and copied out passages from what he was reading. I am impressed by the range of his reading: he quotes William James in *The Varieties of Religious Experience*; there are lines from Walt Whitman, Sybille Bedford, M.F.K. Fisher, T.S. Eliot, Henry Miller. He lists novels by George Orwell, Thomas Mann, D.H. Lawrence's *The Plumed Serpent* ("I still enjoy it"), Norman Mailer's *The Deer Park*. He was fascinated by E.E. Cummings, again someone he admired in breaking away from formal conventions.

On one page I find these lines of Cummings:

> While you and i have lips and voices which are for kiss-
> ing and to sing with who cares if some one-eyed son of
> a bitch invents an instrument to measure spring with

And also this from E.B. White, writing in the *New Yorker* in the McCarthy era:

> Democracy is itself a religious faith. For some it comes
> close to being the only formal religion they have. And
> so when I see the first faint shadow of orthodoxy sweep
> across the sky, feel the first cold whiff of its blinding fog
> steal in from the sea, I tremble all over, as though I had
> just seen an eagle go by, carrying a baby.

He pasted scraps of drawings into the logbook, and the postcards he so loved. There were photographs of friends and of
people he admired, artists like Picasso, Hemingway, Pollock,
a prizefighter named Sam Langford, Babe Ruth and Michael
Romanoff, or just some nameless, evocative face.

The traditional captain's logbook became his canvas, a space
beyond the tight little correspondence cards where he could let
his imagination, his wit, and his sense of style play freely without

On board the Zuleika Dobson, *from FPK's logbook, c. 1954*

constraint. The *Zuleika Dobson* failed as a boating experience but served my father well as a reminder of what he wanted in his life: the bold freedom of the artist.

I have surrendered my role as the one to make my parents happy by being the "good girl." The old cliché is right: we are who we are and I accept. I try to be the listener as my mother was, and I prize my father's tease of a warning not to grow stuffy in my old age. Once in New York City, looking out the window of my apartment through the gauzy haze of early spring bloom, I saw from a distance a stately procession of elephants lumbering quietly by. It seemed a mirage, but then I realized it was part of the annual rite of the Ringling Brothers Circus menagerie arriving from Florida on their way to Madison Square Garden. I was delighted to catch sight of them even if they did not belong in Central Park.

In the same way, in my memory, far off, I see two thoughtful, uncertain people, not so sure of themselves but always saved by their sense of humor. There is a grave, attentive mother, holding her middle daughter in a stiff embrace as she teaches her the box step while she hums off-key the tune of her girlhood, "Night and day, day and night." And there is a puckish, green-eyed father, surrounded by his stubby tubes of oil paints, working on those crisp note cards from the Porcellian Club stationery box but taking time out to write his absent daughter:

> Have fun, be curious, and then come home.
> We miss you but are glad you are seeing things.